AFRICAN ADVENTURES

Mother and daughter on the alert

AFRICAN ADVENTURES

by

John F. Burger

ILLUSTRATED

SAFARI PRESS, INC.

P.O. BOX 3095, Long Beach, CA 90803

AFRICAN ADVENTURES by John F. Burger. Special contents of this edition copyright © 1993 SAFARI PRESS, INC. All inquiries should be addressed to: Safari Press, Inc., P.O. Box 3095, Long Beach, CA 90803, U.S.A.

Burger, John F.

ISBN 0-940143-77-1

10 9 8 7 6 5 4 3 2 1

This is the 36th book published by Safari Press.

CONTENTS

FOREWORD

African Adventures has been written mainly in response to the request of those friendly readers of my previous book, *African Buffalo Trails*, who asked for more fare of a similar nature. These were the readers who joined me on one of the branch roads of adventure which took us to the Kivu, the Ituri Forest and the Ubangi—the native haunts of the gorilla, the pygmy and the cannibal.

In the present volume we return to the main road which starts in the desolate Karoo country and leads through the Kalahari Desert, the Back Congo, and on to the Lupa Goldfield in Tanganyika, where some of the strangest characters imaginable become fellow travellers. It is here that we meet a motley crowd, drawn from every strata of society, and the search for the elusive yellow metal takes us, on a black and eerie night, to the grave of an old native queen where a hoard of gold lies buried beside her.

On another side road we accompany the world's most fantastic snake-man and see him capture and take bites from the deadly mamba and cobra. In the dense forest of the cannibal we sit at night and listen to the savage drummers sending out their messages, which we interpret successfully.

On Christmas Eve we sit around the camp-fire in the vast open plains and sing Christmas carols with the blacks whilst the music is provided by a celebrated artist. On yet another night we sit and listen to intimate stories about the most famous hunters who have passed over the African hunting scene. And once again we share adventures on the trail of the lion, the elephant, and the buffalo.

Although to some extent biographical, the adventures I have recorded here are not in chronological order, but I have presented them in a sequence which I hope will afford pleasure and excitement to readers as they follow me on the many different trails.

JOHN F. BURGER.

Palma de Mallorca.
February 8th, 1957.

CHAPTER I

EARLY DAYS ON THE GREAT KAROO

I WAS BORN ON a farm in the Prieska district, a town many miles out on the Backveld on the fringes of the Great Karoo. Thinking it over seriously, I feel convinced that to have been born on the Karoo Backveld at the time of which I write was a major disaster, and no serious person, given the choice, would ever have elected to make his first appearance in that part of the world, for I was thus condemned later to farm life on the Karoo for several years before Providence eventually took a hand and came to the rescue.

That Providence should have bestirred itself on my account, even though belatedly, seems rather strange, for if the records I have perused are reliable, it would appear that from the earliest time of its recorded history the Karoo has harboured one branch or another of the Burger family. As a child, I remember the little town of Burgerville—named after my forebears—and not so long before I made my appearance in those parts an uncle of mine, Ben Burger, had the misfortune to get himself mixed up in one of the interminable squabbles with the Karoo Bushmen of that time. Uncle Ben was unlucky enough to get in the way of a poisoned arrow. A rough cross, far out on the Karoo, marks the place where he relinquished all further interest in the Bushman troubles.

At the time I made my appearance the Bushman episode was nearing its end, but there were still intermittent skirmishes in different parts of the country, and we often received news that some farmer or other had had the good fortune to ' bag a Bushman '. In those days this diminutive nomadic tribe were still legitimate prey, and if ever they were indiscreet enough to get within the range of the old ' *voorlaaiers* ' (blunderbusses) of the Karoo farmer, they were bagged in much the same way as the modern hunter bags his game trophy today. That the Bushmen were themselves to a large extent responsible for this campaign of extermination is probably true. I have never read the Bushmen's view of the matter, but the Karoo farmer of those days believed that there was no other way to settle the trouble.

Our farm was named 'Welgevonden', which, literally translated, means 'Lucky Strike'. I have never been able to discover what it was that made that dump a lucky strike. All I ever struck there was misery, and plenty of it. It has often been said, and with justification, that farmers on the Backveld could look out of their front doors on a Monday morning and tell correctly what visitors they were likely to have the following Saturday night. On Welgevonden we could tell the movements of visitors a fortnight ahead. In fact, we never had any visitors at all, so it did not make any serious difference.

Our farm was typical of many others on the Great Karoo— the vast, flat plains where nothing but the karoo bush grows. The karoo bush is a succulent plant which rarely exceeds 8 inches in height, but it has the most amazing drought-resisting qualities and is the sole source of nourishment for millions of sheep on the Karoo. On Welgevonden farm we lived a life of complete isolation, for the automobile had not yet made its appearance, and the donkey provided the only means of transport. Farmers in those parts occupied themselves in looking after their own interests, which consisted mainly in the breeding of sheep, ostriches, and donkeys. The distances separating the farms were so great, and the means of transport so slow, that it was rare indeed for them to visit each other. Our family made contact with the outside world on the rare occasions when it was necessary to visit the nearest town, 100 miles away, in order to procure foodstuffs in sufficient quantities to last for three or more months. Then back to the living grave, Welgevonden, where, like all other farmers, we bred sheep, ostriches, and donkeys. These animals are not noted for their intelligence or reasoning powers, and that probably explains why they flourished so well on the Great Karoo when food and water were obtainable. But it often happened that food and water were completely unobtainable as a result of prolonged droughts.

One of my earliest memories on the farm was of a period of severe drought. I was fully five years of age before the first rain fell on Welgevonden. In the years preceding this memorable event our flocks of sheep diminished daily. Often a hundred or more carcasses were collected in one day and piled in a heap to be devoured by the ubiquitous jackal. But even these scavengers can have a surfeit of mutton, and when that happened the stench around the farm was unbearable. We never employed sufficient labourers to bury so many dead animals, and on the Karoo firewood is non-existent. The best we could do was to drag the carcasses to a central point, where they were left to decay.

Water—or rather the lack of it—was an ever-present and menacing problem. Then there was the one year when an already hopeless situation was aggravated by the mass migration of millions of springboks. During the course of a few days hundreds of thousands of these animals over-ran our farm and laid the country bare. Their approach to the farm could be heard miles away, and a dense column of dust marked their advance. By the time the herd had passed over our farm the country was completely barren. We ourselves escaped being trampled to death by sitting indoors and watching thousands upon thousands of animals rampaging over the farm. An enclosure surrounding the well from which we drew our drinking-water was flattened out, and after the herd had gone the well was filled to the top with dead and dying animals. Hundreds of sheep and lambs were trampled to death and many hundreds more disappeared before the moving mass.

It was not long after this catastrophe that rain fell in our part of the Karoo. In an incredibly short time the karoo bush began to sprout, and brought relief to the remnants of our flock of sheep, which had been reduced from some 5,000 head to a meagre 2,000. A few weeks later another disaster overtook us, when we experienced a terrific hailstorm. Hailstones the size of pigeon eggs beat down in relentless fury. After the storm hail lay several inches deep, and hundreds of sheep had perished. These disasters were prevalent all over the Karoo, and no one was immune from the trail of misery and distress occasioned by drought, hail, and springbok depredations. As time went on the springbok migrations became rarer and less intensive. The mass migration I saw as a child was probably the last in which millions of animals were involved.   Subsequent migrations were on a smaller scale, and not so widely spread.

For a while life went on tranquilly enough, then, suddenly, another disaster—perhaps the greatest of all—overtook us.   We awoke one morning to find our country at war with England. On our lonely farm at the beginning of operations we were not unduly disturbed by this event, but as the struggle continued we were inevitably drawn into the vortex, and it was not very long before my Father was commandeered by the Boers to present himself for military service.   It was whilst we were on our way to Britstown, where Father had to register, that we were captured by a British regiment under the command of a Colonel Scovell.   I was too young to remember many of the details of this incident, but thirty-five years later the managing director of a gold-mining company in Tanganyika Territory, of which I was then the secretary, paid an official visit to the property, and Colonel Scovell and I were fated to meet for a second time.   Although I remembered much less than he did about our first meeting, we had several interesting conversations together, and before his departure the Colonel was kind enough to offer me a responsible position in their organization overseas.   I could choose between Europe, China, and Australia.   After much serious consideration I decided to remain where I was.   I have no doubt that my decision was a wise one, for three years later we were at war with Nazi Germany. But I am going far ahead of my story.

After the termination of the Boer War we once again returned to Welgevonden, where, as a child, my activities on the farm were devoted to scouring the country in search of stray lambs—a peaceful enough occupation normally.   But the peace and quiet of the countryside were often rudely disturbed during the ostrich mating season.   The male birds then became aggressive and resented the presence of humans. On these occasions they were extremely dangerous, and often attacked without provocation.   There are hundreds of instances recorded on the Karoo of people who have been killed by male ostriches.   I learned early in life that the best defence against a charging ostrich was to get down to a prone position at the first sign of danger.   In this position the bird was prevented from doing serious damage with its feet, and it would then resort to pecking or sitting on top of its intended victim. A sharp stroke across the neck with a heavy cane quickly cured it of its aggressive tendencies.

I intensely disliked male ostriches, and had a horror of being pecked or trampled upon whilst lying flat on the ground. One morning, when fossicking in a store-room, I came across a bar of round iron. In appearance it differed very little from the cane I usually carried, but in the matter of weight there was a vast difference. I determined to discard the cane and use in its place the rod of iron. With such a weapon I could emphasize my dislike of the ostrich much more effectively. That day I successfully killed three male ostriches, and the next day the stage was set for an all-out campaign against any aggressive male, when Dad suddenly appeared on the scene. He still carried a heavy cane, and with it he promptly emphasized his dislike of seeing the birds killed—on my posterior.

During the plucking season the males were not at all dangerous and were usually driven into large kraals along with the females, where they were denuded of their best plumes. The plucking was generally done early in the mornings, after which they were set free to scrounge for food—ostriches will eat anything, from mealie seeds to ironmongery. On letting them loose my father often retained one bird, and after the flock had walked a mile or more, he would lift me on to its back and set it free to join its companions. There is a serious division of opinion as to whether the ostrich could ever fly or not. Judging by the speed at which he can cover the ground on his two legs, I do not believe it was ever necessary for any ostrich to resort to flight. The Karoo can be bitterly cold in the early mornings, and I often thought I would freeze to death, seated on the back of an ostrich stepping it out at the rate of 40 to 50 miles an hour. Apart from the bitter cold, there was always the possibility that the bird's all-out effort to join the flock would end in sudden collapse. This actually happened on a number of occasions, and I considered myself lucky to find my way back home with nothing worse than a severe shaking and with all my bones intact. Whatever amusement this ostrich-riding business may have afforded the onlookers, it only intensified my hatred of the creature.

But this was only a passing phase. Years later, when I had

B

taken to the hunting business, I met hundreds of wild ostriches in the bush, but nothing could ever persuade me to kill one of them.

I had now reached the age of nine. Each successive day seemed to bring more work and hardship, and I had long since formed an active dislike of the farm and all it stood for; but there was no apparent escape from it all, and reluctantly I settled down to the life, always hoping that something or other would happen to liberate me from it. Little did I know that liberation was so close at hand and that it would come in such tragic circumstances.

One bitter night in winter I accompanied my father to search for stray lambs. It was just one more outing like so many others before, and I had no reason to suppose that it would be the last. We were caught in a blinding storm and returned home very late, drenched and frozen to the bone. Next morning Dad was too ill to leave his bed, and later that day we found that he had contracted double pneumonia. A week later we buried him in a shallow grave, dug by my younger brother, an old Hottentot servant, and myself. The crude setting of this funeral remains one of the most painful memories of my life.

The death of my father soon made it obvious that we would have to abandon the farm. Mother decided to sell out and return to her folks, there to resume her premarital occupation of school-teacher. Three months later all arrangements were completed for our departure to the little town of Strydenburg (Town of Strife) in the Orange Free State. We said good-bye to Welgevonden, and I prayed that it would never be necessary for me to set eyes on the Great Karoo again. My prayer was answered, but I am not so sure now whether I am glad or sorry. Since the time of our departure great changes have swept over the Karoo. As the result of intensive scientific development of the sheep-breeding industry, embracing not only the wool but also the karakul hide, the country has become enormously wealthy. The farmer of today no longer depends on the donkey for his transport. Many of them own their own 'planes, and luxurious motor-cars and trucks ensure rapid movement. Yes, the Karoo has changed since those far-off days, and it must have proved an exciting venture for those who remained behind to build new homes and a new country. As always, my family name is still well represented on the Great Karoo, and they have shared in that great achievement. But for myself, I searched for, and found, adventure of a different kind in countries far from the scene of my early boyhood. It is of these adventures that I would write now.

CHAPTER II

I TAKE TO THE HILLS

L IFE IN S TRYDENBURG differed in many ways from the life in Welgevonden. On the farm I had learned only the rough rudiments of schooling, now the forenoons were devoted to lessons and religious services. Strydenburg was inhabited by a ' dopper ' community, a fanatical religious sect which had its origin in Holland. During weekdays there were generally five religious services, whilst on Sundays the number was stepped up to seven. Often the number exceeded seven; these were the occasions when the preacher would divulge to his flock some information he had gained by Divine intuition or from a newspaper. (In Strydenburg it was only the parson who ever had access to a newspaper, the rest of the flock read the *Kerkbode*, a paper devoted entirely to religion and which appeared fortnightly.)

On one occasion I remember well, circular letters were sent out to the entire district calling for a special day of prayer. The trouble on this occasion was that the preacher had read a newspaper article which described how the tsetse-flies were moving south in Central Africa. He felt certain that ere long Strydenburg would be overrun by tsetses. In the manner of Sodom and Gomorrah, the flock was called upon to pray for immunity from this scourge. It was a question of ' pray or sleep yourself to death '. For weeks special prayers were offered daily, and in the end we finally escaped the plague. At that time none of us knew that sleeping sickness was a centuries-old problem in Central Africa and that it was physically impossible for a tsetse to live on the small Karoo. Years later I spent much of my life in some of the worst tsetse-infected areas in Africa and did most of my hunting on tsetse-control work. Those prayers had nothing whatever to do with stemming of the evil tide.

Strydenburg had three authorities who completely controlled the lives of its citizens: the parson—he controlled everybody, mentally, physically, and spiritually; the post-master, who was also a special Justice of the Peace and acted as magistrate—he sent people to gaol; and the village 'Bobby', who worried everybody and took a fiendish delight in catching young boys who smoked cigarette ends.

Public bars were declared out of bounds to the faithful. The parson ruled this side of social life with an iron fist. He himself never entered a bar, but he paid regular daily visits to an old well at the far end of his property, and every afternoon he could be seen descending it—ostensibly to examine the pump-ing installation. But one afternoon he failed to come to the surface, and later that evening a passer-by heard him calling for help from the bottom of the well. It appeared that the tow-rope he used had snapped and the old man had been badly injured. Help was immediately forthcoming, and a member of the flock quickly descended the well in order to render the neces-sary assistance. On reaching the bottom he was deeply shocked to see a case of brandy carefully hidden away from public view. After this incident pub-crawling was endured with a good deal more tolerance.

I never took kindly to prayer or schooling, and in spite of my early dislike of Welgevonden, I now often longed for the freedom of farm life. The ostriches, the lambs, the flocks of sheep, the excitement of chasing and trapping jackals—town life lacked all these adventures. For Mother, also, life had changed very materially. She had the misfortune to teach what I am now convinced was a band of irredeemable little ruffians of which I soon became a star member. The town at that time sported a European population of about 300, whilst the coloured 'Hottentot' population numbered more than double that figure. Fights and feuds readily developed between us European kids and the young Hottentot fraternity, and before long we had organized ourselves into two active warring factions. Saturday afternoons saw us gather at a big pan near the town. Here, armed with quince-canes and an inex-haustible supply of wet clay which we affixed to the ends of the canes, hostilities would commence at a range of 50 yards. As the intensity of the fighting increased, so the distance separating us decreased, and we usually ended up in a free-for-all hand-to-hand encounter.

On one occasion I shipped the full force and benefit of a mouthful of clay from a distance of 10 yards and a moment later my adversary and I were locked in a life-and-death hand-to-hand struggle.   For some time I was on the receiving end, and things began to look grim, when fate suddenly came to my rescue.   My opponent had landed a particularly savage swing on my jaw, and I was knocked to the ground.   A second later he was on top of me dishing out punishment with both hands.   It was then that I noticed a big rock lying close by. I immediately grabbed this, and in a remarkably short time the fortunes of war had changed, so that I gained top position. Unfortunately I had no means of determining the exact resistance of a Hottentot's skull, and I made full use of the rock. By the time I had settled the score and my companions had dragged me from my victim I had caused the poor fellow serious injury.   By then he was unconscious, and our combined efforts to restore him to life failed entirely.   So here was I, at the age of ten, with the crime of murder on my hands.

This was a serious, and totally unexpected, development, and after long discussion with other members of the gang it was decided that I ' take to the hills '.   There definitely was no point in my returning home and informing Mother that I had committed murder, and then there was also the matter of the town ' Bobby ' to consider.   That night I spent in the hills, also the next two days and nights.   During this time I fed liberally on prickly pears, which grew in profusion all over the hills, and drank from a fresh-water fountain.   But prickly pear is no permanent diet for any man, and by the third day, when a search-party found me hiding behind a rock, I had just about reached the end of my tether.   The bitter cold and the terror animal noises inspired in me made me realize fully that murder is a very serious crime.   It turned out, however, that the Hottentot had been taken to hospital, where he made a rapid recovery.   Mine was a hollow victory indeed.

After this escapade the Saturday afternoon free-for-alls became unpopular.   We soon discovered an old mining-shaft near the town, and here we gathered at week-ends for smoking sessions, hundreds of cigarette ends having been collected during the week for the purpose.   As I have said before, smoking by teen-agers was one of the deadly sins, and the town ' Bobby ' treated it as such. It was whilst I was gathering cigarette ends outside an hotel one afternoon that I felt a heavy hand descend upon me. The ' Cop ' had caught me red-handed in the act, and inside my pockets there was plenty of evidence. I was taken home, where, after pleading guilty to Mother, the hand of the law, armed with a choice quince-cane, descended upon my posterior five times. After that I fixed a pin in the end of a cane and lifted butt-ends without stooping or betraying myself. But we were all suspect, and one afternoon, whilst six of us were sitting smoking at the bottom of the shaft, the ' Cop ' suddenly appeared on the scene. There were hundreds of butt-ends in a tin which we kept for the purpose. The evidence was taken to our respective homes. The hand of the law descended upon me again, and brought to an end one more form of amusement.

In the absence of free fights and smokes, we soon found other forms of amusements—more or less within the law—and life went on merrily enough until one afternoon Mother called my brother and me into her bedroom and informed us that we were soon to have another father. The marriage was duly celebrated, and it quickly became evident to me that I was one too many in the new menage. The smallest misdemeanour or boyish prank brought down the most dire consequences. I hated this interloper who provided more beatings than smiles. ' Old Nick ', as I called him, was the guiding genius of a transport service motivated by donkey power. Frequently I was sent out on long trips which, if they provided little pleasure, saved me from the unwelcome attentions of ' Old Nick '.

On one of these trips I had to accompany the wagons to remove the belongings of a close neighbour who had suddenly come into a fortune by virtue of the sale of some valuable property on the diamond-field at Kimberley. The prize item of his collection of junk was a rough coffin which the old man wanted to take with him in case of emergency. I loathed having this crude home-made casket next to me—especially at night time—and often prayed that the emergency would arise to put it to better use, so that I might be relieved of its presence. The emergency, however, did not arise during the trip, and at the end of nearly three weeks we reached our destination—a small station on the main line near the Orange River. The occasion of our arrival was celebrated that night with the help of a liberal supply of ' dop ' (cheap South African brandy).

Later that night, being the only sober member of the company, I was called upon to escort the old man to his waiting-room at the station.   The sum of ten shillings being the reward I was promised for this service, I gladly accepted.   On arrival at the waiting-room a difficulty arose over the payment, and it was only after a prolonged argument that I finally persuaded the old man of the justice of my cause.   I was asked to enter the room and take down a steel trunk from a shelf on the wall. Assuming that the trunk contained the usual odds and ends required on a journey, I attempted to lift it down.   Its weight, however, was such that I was unable to hold it, and the next instant it crashed to the floor and the contents spilled all over the room.   That case was packed with golden sovereigns and other coins, which I helped to gather up and replace.   I was handed a sovereign and thanked for my help, and with that I left the room. It was only the next morning that I learned that the trunk contained over £3,000 in good coin.   This information was offered by a police officer who came to inquire into the loss of the trunk and its contents.   Our wagons were detained for three days whilst investigations proceeded, but the money was never recovered.

I have often wondered since whether my graphic description of the night's events did not induce a member of the convoy to return to the scene of my surprising discovery.   I have also wondered whether I had not listened to too much hell-fire and brimstone before this occurrence.   Mother was very proud of me when I recounted to her the events of the trip and the part I had played in this affair.   It is, however, a moot point whether a mother's pride exceeds the value of £3,000 in good currency. The fact that my sovereign also mysteriously disappeared before the end of the journey convinces me that one member of that convoy finished up £3,001 richer than he was at the beginning.

There were many more trips over the small Karoo, with varying fortunes, and towards the end of that year ' Old Nick ' decided that there was no future in the transport business in that part of the world.   Preparations were soon being made for a trek by donkey-wagons to Southern Rhodesia, some 1,200 miles away, and the first week in January saw us en route to the new land of promise and wealth.

CHAPTER III

WE TREK NORTH

Nowadays a trip to Cape Town from Bulawayo, by air, can be accomplished in a matter of three hours. By car it is comfortably done in three days. The routes are well mapped, hotels in towns along the road provide first-class comfort, and the journey is looked upon as something in the nature of a joy-ride. But this is 1956. At the beginning of the century conditions were totally different. In those days aeroplanes were still unheard of and roads, for the greater part, were non-existent. The available road-maps were most unreliable and the traveller is not now confronted with the delays inevitably encountered by the straggler of those days, when a distance of 10 miles per day was considered good going.

In preparing for our trek north we had no knowledge of the conditions prevailing beyond the borders of the Union of South Africa. A great deal was taken for granted, and we hoped for the best. Our expedition consisted of only two covered wagons; the provisions we could carry were limited by the amount of space available after allowing for the personal effects of three families consisting of ten persons.

On the way up as far as Kimberley we experienced little difficulty in replenishing stores of foodstuffs and necessities, but from there onwards conditions deteriorated daily. The question of making points at nights where water was obtainable presented us with the greatest of difficulties. Each wagon required fourteen donkeys, and in addition there were eight extras. It was essential that the day's journey should terminate at a point where there was sufficient water for us and our animals. A trek of 10 miles per day is about as much as one can expect from a donkey, but water-holes were often 20 or more miles apart. This meant night and day trekking, and on such occasions the speed would decrease as thirst and fatigue increased. The condition of the animals rapidly deteriorated, and any idea of a time-table had to be abandoned owing to the enforced delays to rest our livestock.   For all that, our progress was reasonably good.   We were still travelling through the sparsely inhabited parts of the Union, there was still the occasional store where we could procure the most essential foodstuffs.

But soon we were to enter Bechuanaland and the Kalahari desert.   Our serious troubles started from the time we left Mafeking.   From this point onwards the road-maps and information as to the existence of water-holes became utterly unreliable.   In the earlier stages we often made points where water was indicated, only to find dry mud-pools.   On these occasions we were forced to camp, drive the donkeys to the next water-hole, and bring them back to the wagons.   The progress was slow and conditions become more impossible each day.   The animals were in poor fettle and grazing was inadequate.

Up to now our troubles were mainly confined to supplies and water, but soon we had to contend with wild animals.   The jackal and the hyena could be heard nightly soon after sunset. We were not greatly disturbed by the sound of the jackal, for on the Karoo he is encountered frequently, but the hyena was an animal of which we knew nothing, and we were alarmed by his eerie cry.   Often they approached the camp-fires closely enough to be seen clearly.   Seated on their haunches, they would send forth their weird, bloodcurdling calls.

This meant that we had to construct shelters at night to secure our donkeys.   More often than not, the necessary bushes from which to construct shelters were unobtainable, and on these occasions a native guard, armed with an ancient Martini-Henry, was posted on duty.   Apart from their continuous wailing, the hyenas never molested our livestock.   This was just as well, for little reliance can be placed upon a native in the face of danger from wild animals.

The trying conditions under which we laboured were extremely fatiguing, and in spite of the piercing cries of the hyenas and jackals, we managed to sleep well at nights.   But soon we were to be deprived of even this comfort.   Whilst we were round the camp-fire one night there was a terrific roar quite close to our camp.   It was the first occasion on which any of us had ever heard the roar of a lion. To sit in an arm-chair and listen to a lion roaring in a menagerie is a fascinating experience which most people thoroughly enjoy. In my later days, when I had made hunting my profession, the absence of a lion roaring in the distance—or even close to camp at night—was a keen disappointment. There were the many nights when I sat up waiting for them and looked forward to an en-counter with the keenest anticipation. But the circumstances then were different; I had learned to know all that was worth knowing about the King of Beasts, and I was equipped to meet him on something like equal terms. Out here on the Kalahari, with our meagre equipment and a complete lack of experience, it was a terrifying ordeal.

We dreaded the nights, and every strange sound in the dark filled us with terror. Our donkeys had never previously heard or seen a lion, but when that big brute went into vocal action that first night they all vanished in a matter of seconds—where the lion is concerned all animals are guided by an unerring instinct: those donkeys were well endowed with instinct and they vacated the scene in a great hurry. There were no volunteers in our party to offer to round them up again that night, and when the lion finally ceased exercising his vocal chords we went off to sleep, firmly convinced that the rest of our journey would have to be accomplished on foot. Later in life I learned to know that a roaring lion is seldom danger-ous, and that happened to be the case on this occasion. For the next two days we scoured the country in search of our absconding donkeys. It was late on the afternoon of the second day that we had them all finally rounded up and safely back in camp. The lions on this occasion were apparently not at-tracted by the poor fare offered by two spans of emaciated donkeys.

But this was only the beginning. Farther on our trek north they were not so discriminating. The fact of their presence, however, immediately added to our difficulties. Our concern now was not only to find water and green branches to build shelters at the end of each day's trek: we also had to find ample firewood with which to build fires at night. We were still ignorant enough to believe that a fire at night would prove a deterrent to a hungry lion. But on this point we were speedily disillusioned.   Whilst sitting round the camp-fire one night there was a terrific snarl, and this was followed immediately by the appearance of a huge male lion.   He was in no way deterred by the fire, or by our presence, and before we could recover from our shock he had departed, dragging with him one of our donkeys.   In our scant equipment we carried no shooting lamps, and even had we done so, I doubt very much whether any member of our party would have risked his skin to save that unfortunate beast.   Before the night was over we had a second visitation and parted company with donkey No. 2.   It became painfully obvious that at this rate of destruction our trek would soon come to an inglorious end. The situation had become alarming, and our nerves suffered accordingly.   It was bad enough to lose one or more donkeys each night in order to appease the lions' appetites; but what was to happen to us when the supply of donkeys became exhausted?   Henceforth we were compelled to erect broader and higher fences round the animals and, generally, we found that where there was ample bush for this purpose there was no water, and vice versa.   Our trek, begun with so much hope and confidence, was rapidly heading for complete disaster.

A few days after the experience with the lions we suffered another major disaster, when one of the wagon-shafts was broken. It was nearly a week before the damage could be repaired, and during this period we were menaced nightly by lions.   Our provisions were almost exhausted and at our present rate of progress it would be several days before we would reach one of the widely scattered stores on the desert—a place named Gaberonnes.   Here we met an old transport contractor who had been in the district some years, and the picture he painted of conditions farther north filled us with alarm.   He, himself, had two enormous scars across one of his cheeks.   These, he explained, were caused by a python.   It appeared that whilst out hunting one day he had taken refuge from the blazing sun under a big tree where, after a while, he dropped off to sleep.   He was awakened by the snake gathering him up in its coils.   Fortunately the top section of his body was still free, and he grabbed his rifle, which was lying near him.   In the next instant the snake had encircled the hand in which he held the rifle.   It was in this desperate position that he managed to manœuvre his finger on to the trigger, and he was lucky to sever the spinal cord of the reptile, which then retaliated by fastening its fangs in his cheek. The wounds turned septic and he was removed to hospital at Mafeking, where he lay in a critical condition for several weeks.

A few weeks before our arrival, a black mamba had lodged itself in a branch suspended over a footpath along which his trek-oxen walked daily. Six oxen were accounted for as they walked in single file below the deadly serpent. Some days later I was scouting for honey and pulled away the branches in front of a cavity in a large tree-trunk. As I cleared the last bit of foliage, I looked into the eyes of a monster-size python. I have always regretted that there was no one in the vicinity to time me over the first 100 yards.

Some two weeks after we left Gaberonnes we arrived late one night at a spot where, according to our map, there was a water-hole. At some time in the distant past there may have been water at this spot, but on our arrival there we found nothing but a dried-up mud-pool. This was an alarming discovery. We ourselves, and also our donkeys, had been without water for more than twenty-four hours. If the road map could be relied upon, the next water-hole was more than 20 miles away. The animals were completely parched and exhausted, and to pull their loads for yet another 20 miles was quite beyond their physical resources. That night we hardly slept at all; we were depressed and alarmed at the unenviable situation in which we found ourselves.

Early the next morning we reviewed the situation carefully, and it was decided that we should fan out in pairs on the different footpaths leading across the country in the hope that one of them might lead us to water. I accompanied Stomp, an old Hottentot driver, who had worked for us for many years. Stomp had an uncanny way with animals—especially donkeys—but early in life he took a violent dislike to any other form of work. He intensely disliked walking, and with the parching thirst he was suffering at the time, it was not long before he decided that he had had enough. There were faint signs of footprints of a comparatively recent date, and I felt convinced that if we followed these they would lead us to water or some habitation. Stomp, however, was not impressed with my reasoning and refused to continue. It was obvious that he had reached a stage where it was impossible to stir up any enthusiasm in him, and in view of his determination to call it a day, I decided to carry on alone.

As I continued on the path, more and more signs of recent footprints became evident. The country was completely flat; here and there small patches of short brush were dotted along the path. I could see a long way ahead, and after another hour's walk I saw a man approaching me in the distance. My spirits rose, and in spite of my thirst and fatigue, I accelerated my pace so as to meet up with this straggler at the earliest possible moment. He was now less than a mile away; in a few minutes he might be able to help me quench my thirst or direct me to the nearest water. Now only a few hundred yards separated us—the time of deliverance was at hand—only a few more yards . . . and then, suddenly, a menacing snarl, as a huge male lion emerged from a clump of bushes at the side of the path. The man was knocked to the ground, where he was seized and shaken in much the same manner as a cat would shake a mouse, and then dragged into the cluster of bush from where the lion had rushed upon him. That native must have been killed with the first stroke, for I never heard him utter a sound.

I was petrified with fear, and expected the lion to return and attack me at any moment. Suddenly I became hysterical and cried bitterly. I prayed to God to save me from the terrible fate of the native I had seen dragged into the bush. At the ripe old age of ten years an experience such as this can be a very distressing affair. Fear rooted me to the spot from which I had watched the tragedy. I did not know then that the lion only rarely kills wantonly, and that his killing is dictated by the demands of his stomach or by aggravation. I felt convinced that as soon as he had devoured the native he would return to collect me. I had no weapon with which to defend myself, and there was no tree in the vicinity to which I could look for safety. I was suffering agonizing thirst, my feet were aching, and I was weary to death. I had not sufficient energy left in me even to try to run, and in any case, running would not avail me much against a hungry lion. The situation seemed desperate to me, and just how long I stood there rooted to the ground, weeping and praying for help, I do not know.

Finally I began to calm down. The lion had not reappeared, and I believed that he had gone a long distance to devour his victim. Actually he was less than 100 yards from me all this time—a fact we discovered some days later when we returned to the scene of the tragedy and found only a few bones on the spot where the native was devoured. At last I mustered enough courage to proceed on my way. At the spot where the lion had attacked his victim I found a clasp-knife, a pipe with a broken stem, and a small bag which contained some native tobacco—pathetic souvenirs, which I kept for many years. At the moment my greatest concern was to get as far away as possible from that spot. I set off at a brisk pace and stuck to the footpath, and made wide detours wherever there was any brush in the vicinity of the path.

It was now well past mid-day, and I was suffering even more acutely from thirst and fatigue, and although I had eaten nothing since early that morning, I did not feel hungry. When thirst predominates, one is insensible to almost every other need. By now I was walking almost mechanically, but some distance ahead I could see a big tree—large enough to protect me from the sun and any lions that might be prowling about. When finally I reached the tree I was at the end of my physical resources. My hopes were, however, once again doomed to disappointment, for the tree was too large for me to climb and the lowest branches were well beyond my reach. But there was ample shade from the sun, and even the fear of lions could not induce me to move from this shelter. I had hardly sat down when I fell into a deep sleep, from which I awoke late in the afternoon. In less than an hour the sun would go down, and I became alarmed when I thought of the dangers that threatened me.

I decided to follow the path where more and more fresh footprints began to show. As the sun was setting I came to a stop. The position seemed completely hopeless; I was too tired and thirsty to continue walking, and the thought of a night alone in the open terrified me. I was still standing turning things over in my mind when suddenly a native drum started beating in the distance. That sound was music to my ears, and fatigue and thirst suddenly seemed to vanish. I followed the sound of the drum, and as darkness began to fall

I walked into a small native kraal. It was a timely deliverance, for I was then on the point of collapse.

The natives were obviously surprised at seeing a European child walking into their kraal at that time of night—more so in view of the fact that I could not speak their language or make myself understood. I could, however, make them understand that I was thirsty, and an old native, apparently the head of the community, attended to my needs; he allowed me only a few mouthfuls of water at intervals. Later I was given maize-meal to eat. They seemed greatly perturbed at my presence and there were long discussions, of which I understood nothing. At the end of the parley four natives appeared with a *masheila*, and the old man signalled for me to get into it.

All sorts of fears assailed me. My previous experience with blacks was limited to the Hottentots on the Karoo, who all spoke our language. On the farm and in Strydenburg I had often heard stories of the savagery of the natives in the north. For all I knew, I was being taken to a place of execution. Their demeanour, however, seemed friendly, and I resigned myself to my fate. Some hours after we left this small kraal we arrived at a large native village and I was taken to a big, well-built, modern house, where I was ushered into the presence of the head of the community—King Khama. At the time I spoke very little English, and the Bechuana language was completely foreign to me, but by means of signs I managed to make the King understand that our convoy was stranded miles away without water. I was provided with a sumptuous meal and given a comfortable bed for the night, and early next morning a party of natives was sent out to find the wagons and guide them to the village. It was late the next day when the wagons arrived at Khama's village.

During our enforced stay at the mud-pool a number of donkeys had mysteriously disappeared. They had obviously been stolen by some of the tribesmen. Khama took a serious view of this, and scouts were sent out immediately to recover the animals. Two days later they were returned to us. By this time an interpreter had arrived on the scene, and I gave a full account of the lion incident. There were no hunters in our party, and although scouts went out daily in search of the man-

eater, they failed to find him—it appeared that he had previously accounted for several other natives in the district.

My absence from camp for two days and a night had caused
everyone serious concern. Stomp had returned on the afternoon of the first day, to all intents and purposes completely
paralysed in both legs—a story no one believed. It is true,
though, that had it not been for the lengthy argument we
engaged in that day, before I finally set out on my own, I
should have arrived at the spot where the lion was lying waiting
much sooner than I did, and I would in that case have suffered
the fate of that unfortunate victim.

We remained at Khama's village for more than a week, and
during all that time we were treated with the greatest consideration. It was small consolation for all of us to learn that
during the period we were stuck at the mud-hole we were
actually within a few miles of a pool of fresh water; but this, of
course, we did not then realize. At the end of our stay at Khama's
kraal we were all in much better shape, mentally and physically, and the condition of our animals had greatly improved.

When we left the village Khama provided us with a guide
and instructions to his people that we were to be assisted in
every way possible on our journey through his country.
Twenty years later, whilst in Southern Rhodesia, we were all
grieved to hear of the death of King Khama—a great king and
one of nature's gentlemen. He lived to be ninety-three years old.

Our journey from Khama's village to Francistown, near the
Southern Rhodesian border, a distance of roughly 150 miles,
proved much easier. The help of an experienced guide was of
great value and we were relieved of the worry of finding water.
The country was quite densely populated, and small native
villages dotted the road at regular intervals. At one large
water-pool we came to we found a vast collection of bones and
skulls—mostly buffalo. They were the relics of the great
rinderpest epidemic of 1897. It was, incidentally, my first
encounter with the African buffalo. I did not know then that
later on a great deal of my life would be devoted to the hunting
of this animal. The adventures on that trail I have related
elsewhere.

At Francistown we had further trouble when a number of
donkeys strayed and could not be found for some days. Finally

c

I caught up with them one morning and managed to secure a mount. Whilst driving the remainder back to camp there suddenly came a wild snort and the animals scattered in all directions. The alarm on this occasion was caused by a pack of wild dogs, and for the first time I looked back with gratitude on those ostrich-riding experiences. Had it not been for them, I should never have retained my seat during that wild rush through the bush. Luckily the camp was not far away, and we lost only one donkey to the pack. At this point the guide left us to return to his village.

The rest of the trek from Francistown to Bulawayo, a distance of about 140 miles, was completed in a little under three weeks. When, finally, we reached Bulawayo, we had been on the road for four months and twenty-five days. With rare exceptions that trek from Mafeking northwards was a veritable nightmare experience. Some thirty-five years later I had occasion to cover most of that road again, but this time the journey took only three days and was accomplished in a modern, comfortable motor-car. I have nothing to write about this trip.

CHAPTER IV

EARLY RHODESIAN ADVENTURES

At the time of our arrival in Southern Rhodesia, Bulawayo, now a city with a population of nearly 100,000 inhabitants, was only a small village. The gold-mining industry was still in its infancy, and transport was at a premium. There was plenty of work for a contractor with two wagons, and our organization was soon working at top speed. I was put to school, but most of the daylight hours after school were spent in helping to load wagons and similar chores. Evenings were devoted to home-work and studies.

During week-ends and holidays I always accompanied the wagons on any trips out of town. Once I joined a Selous expedition which lasted for more than six weeks; on another occasion it was a trip with the famous van Rooyen, of ' Bring-Them-Back-Alive ' fame. In this manner I picked up a lot of bush experience, and hunting soon got into my blood. Game was plentiful all over Rhodesia in those days and one had not to go far to find even elephants. My first big-game trophy was a sable antelope which I stalked to within a few yards and brought down with a shot-gun.

At school I took up boxing, and made excellent progress; the game had a natural appeal for me, as it has for any healthy boy. But even at that early stage I was already visualizing the day when I would be able to protect myself against my stepfather, whose dislike of me seemed to grow as time went on and often found expression in outbursts of physical violence. Nowadays when children misbehave themselves a psychiatrist or psychologist is called in to rectify what is looked upon as a form of maladjustment. When I was a child psychiatry was unheard of, and psychology was not very popular with parents —least of all with ' Old Nick ', who believed implicitly in making the necessary adjustments with the aid of a quince-cane. His method was undoubtedly very effective, but the trouble was that he applied it too frequently and on the smallest provocation. It was for this reason that I considered boxing would be a quite useful adjunct to my other education.

My keenness at the time was stimulated by one of our European drivers who had previously been a contender for the South African middle-weight title. He taught me lots of the finer points of the game, and my progress was such that at the end of two years ' Old Nick ' must have looked upon it as a menace to his own well-being, and he forthwith forbade me to have any more to do with the game. Normally I would probably have bowed to his decision, but at the time I was competing in the annual school championships and had already entered the finals. I was determined not to lose an opportunity of winning a title, but ' Old Nick ' had decided against it, and warned me that if I persisted in carrying out my intentions I would be put out on the streets. I did not for a moment believe that he would carry out his threat, but when I returned home late that Saturday night the proud winner of my first title, I found all the doors locked against me.

That night I slept in an outhouse, and early next morning came the showdown. I was left in no doubt that I was out for keeps; the break was final, and not even mother's pleadings were of any avail. I had only recently passed my fourteenth birthday and the situation held very little appeal. Later that day I managed to find temporary quarters with friends in town, and the following day I started work as an apprentice compositor on the town's only newspaper. The starting salary was fifteen shillings per week, and the room I occupied cost ten shillings per week. Although a shilling was worth a lot more in those days than it is today, I soon found it impossible to survive for seven days on five shillings. It frequently happened that the demands of the inner man were so pressing that there was not sufficient left to pay the full rent bill for the week. This state of affairs persisted for some time when, one week, as the result of some reckless eating, there was practically nothing left for the rent. The landlord took up an uncompromising attitude towards my extravagance and explained that he had reached the end of his patience, and once again I was unceremoniously bundled out into the streets.

During the ensuing weeks life on occasion became a very grim business. Mother helped all she could, but as I was able to contact her on only very rare occasions, it did not amount to much.   Salvation came in the shape of an old park near town. Here one could settle down under the massive trees, rent free. Apart from the cold at nights, it served the purpose well, and there was more money for food.

But the nights in the park were by no means as unpleasant as one might be led to believe.   There were many other misfits who found sanctuary there.   This community consisted mainly of remittance men out from England—young men whose conduct made them unwelcome guests in their homes, as a result of which their parents had sent them out to the newest of the British colonies to rehabilitate themselves and save their families from unpleasantness.   They were a reckless, cosmopolitan crowd who could never make ends meet on the allowances they received, and a spell in the park would help them to tide over their difficulties until the next allowance arrived.   They were, for the greater part, well-educated men. At nights we read Darwin, Huxley, Voltaire, Paine, Haeckel, Ingersoll, and all the controversial literature of the period, with the aid of kerosene lamps.   I became an avid reader and listener and the influence my companions exercised upon me in this respect prompted me to greater study, in which their assistance proved of immense value to me.   Soon I joined the technical college in town, where I attended classes three times weekly, and at the police gymnasium I was allowed to join the boxing section.   This ' in-and-out ' life lasted for more than two years, and I look upon it as the most valuable experience of my life.

In the intervening time there had been several augmentations in my salary; at college I had won a scholarship, which, unfortunately, was of no use to me in view of my precarious financial background.   But in boxing I continued to make good progress, and shortly after my seventeenth birthday I joined the professional ranks.   With my increased salary and the money I earned in the ring, my position was greatly improved, and there was no more need for me to resort to the park, except for the purpose of visiting old friends.

I had by now served five years as a printer's devil, and my application to join the editorial staff was accepted.   In this new branch of newspaper work there were many opportunities for general study, as I had access to all books in the reference library, and I read all the worth-while biographies on the shelves.   Looking back on it all now, I am convinced that my experiences in the park and as a journalist were among the most valuable of my life.

My first scoop as a journalist was an unforgettable experience.   It happened after twelve o'clock one night, when the paper had gone to press and I was returning home.   As I was passing an hotel two shots rang out in rapid succession.   I immediately rushed to the scene of the disturbance, where an irate husband had found one of the town's most prominent men occupying the wrong bed.   Both the shots had missed the target, and there was a great deal of shouting and shuffling, from which I gathered sufficient material to write what I considered would be a front-page sensation.   But that article never saw the light of day.   It was years later, after I had joined the select company of ' franc millionaires ' in the Belgian Congo, that I again met this prominent citizen.   He was then trying to force a deal on me which did not appeal to me, and in the end he so irritated me that I decided it would be a good time to remind him of our first meeting.   The reminder had the desired effect, and I was rid of an insufferable bore.   He was, of course, unaware of the fact earlier that I was the reporter who made that famous ' scoop ' which must have cost him a great deal to suppress.

During all these years Rhodesia had been expanding rapidly, and at Que Que, a gold mine some 200 miles from Bulawayo, an important township had sprung up.   A printing works had been started there, at which I decided to try my luck.   It was a happy move, for I became absorbed in the mining industry, where I worked eight hours daily, and at night I was able to fill in three hours as a compositor.   At this stage I was doing better financially than I had ever done before.   Here, also, I met one of the many strange characters it has been my good fortune to know.   This was Ozaka, who at that time claimed the world's bantam-weight jiu-jitsu title.   Ozaka was an Englishman—Stephens—whose parents had emigrated to Japan when he was still a child.   There he learned jiu-jitsu to such good purpose that he eventually beat the best men in that country at their own game.   In those days jiu-jitsu was not very popular outside Japan, and the world tour Ozaka had organized came to grief when he landed at Que Que. Here we soon became intimate friends and shared quarters. Ozaka never weighed much more than 100 lb., but he was the most explosive hundred-weight of live material I ever saw.

His uncanny ability can be judged from a letter he wrote to me from Aldershot in the early stages of the First World War. In it he tells how he pinned Bombardier Billy Wells, then British heavy-weight boxing champion, in less than three minutes. During the six months we shared quarters we practised jiu-jitsu almost daily. Just how many times I was rubbed on the floor during those six months I will never know, but in the end I became quite proficient at the game. Ozaka came to a tragic end, for he was killed in action in France in 1916.

But this happy state of affairs did not last long. War-clouds were banking up, and in August 1914 the First World War brought an end to it all. I joined up with a column which saw service on the borders of Rhodesia and German East Africa. For the next three years I followed the fluctuations of fortune in that long-drawn-out campaign. My old love of hunting again asserted itself, and I managed to obtain an appointment to hunt and supply meat for the front-line troops and porters. It was a hard life, but it provided plenty of excitement and adventure. It was as a result of these adventures that I determined to stick to the hunting game after the end of the war. Even at that early stage the buffalo attracted me more than any other animal in the bush. My first encounter with a buffalo in the field had taken place several years earlier, and as so many readers of *African Buffalo Trails* have written to ask me why I have so persistently made this animal my object, the story is worth relating here.

It happened one week-end whilst I was still at school. An old friend of the family, Cilliers, had organized a week-end hunt, which I accompanied. Early one morning we got on to the trail of buffalo; we soon came up with the herd, and Cilliers selected a big bull, at which he fired. The bull was badly wounded and immediately made for close bush, where it disappeared. Cilliers decided to follow it, and I was all set to accompany him when he turned round and explained to me just how dangerous a mission we were on and insisted that I got myself out of danger by climbing a large tree nearby. He would have done well to follow his own advice, for the warning he gave me were the last words he ever spoke. I had hardly got settled in a big branch high off the ground when two more shots rang out in rapid succession. There was a vicious grunt, and in the next instant two natives who had accompanied Cilliers came rushing for the tree. They had seen the bull closing in on Cilliers and tossing him. They were convinced that he had been killed.

It was several hours later before one of them mustered up enough courage to go down and investigate. A few minutes later he returned to report that Cilliers was dead indeed, and only a few yards from his body was the carcass of the dead bull. It was a frightful experience so early in life, and for a long time I sat pondering over the vindictiveness of an animal that could kill with such ferocity. Cilliers had been tossed on at least three occasions, as was evidenced by the ghastly wounds where the horns had entered, and in addition, his skull had been reduced to a pulp by the massive hooves. It was during those minutes that I sat looking at the mutilated corpse that a longing for revenge overtook me. It was only a childish thought, but the feeling persisted for years.

When, finally, I decided to settle down to the hunting business, that incident kept recurring in my mind and urged me on to the buffalo trail. But as time went on this memory, like so many others, faded from my mind. For all that, Cilliers' death was the incentive that started me on the trail, and having started on it, I found that it offered more excitement and adventure than any other game-trail in Africa. When, at the end of 1947, I decided to call it a day, I had accounted for well over a thousand buffaloes. But the killing was never done vindictively or in a spirit of revenge. The fact is there was nothing in the death of Cilliers that called for revenge. That bull had every right to hit back and settle the score as it thought best. The only fault in the set-up was that Cilliers did not take adequate precautions, and for that lapse —unfortunate though it was—he paid the inevitable price.

During the years in which I totted up my four-figure score, far and away the majority were shot on tsetse-control work, and most of the others in order to provide food in cases of dire necessity. The rest were destroyed because they themselves had turned killer and were a menace at large. It was on the trail of these killers that I experienced some of the most hair-raising adventures during my thirty years of hunting, and I am convinced that it was a generous slice of luck which attended me during all those years on the trail of Kafir Kafir that saved me from a fate similar to the one which overtook Cilliers.

But to return to the East African campaign; a year before the termination of hostilities I was wounded in action. After that my health deteriorated rapidly and I was sent back to Southern Rhodesia for medical treatment.

CHAPTER V

MEET PROFESSOR MORRISEY—WORLD'S GREATEST SNAKE MAN

SHORTLY AFTER MY return to Southern Rhodesia from active service on the Northern Border, I was discharged as medically unfit for further military service. I remained in Bulawayo for about a year, but as the result of recurrence of malaria fever, I was medically advised to settle at the coast for a while.

My next port of call was Durban, where in due course I opened a boxing school and gymnasium, and occasionally tried my luck at promoting fights. For its size, Durban at that time must have harboured more budding world champions than any other city on earth. In a short while some two hundred prospective world-beaters were on the lists. Unfortunately enthusiasm far exceeded ability, and out of this lot only about a dozen showed any real promise, and in order to devote more time and personal attention to them, I later opened a private gymnasium at my home.

One evening, whilst the star performers were going through their paces, there was a knock at the door. Outside stood a youth of some eighteen or nineteen years of age. He had heard about the private gymnasium and was anxious to become a member. I explained to him that strangers were not accepted here but that he could join the school in town. In reply he informed me that the duds in the public school did not interest him, but if I would give him the opportunity, he would undertake to flatten out any boxer I had performing in the private gymnasium.

This was big talk for a youngster standing no more than 5 feet 1 inch and weighing barely 120 lb. At that moment I had three potential South African champions going through their paces, and I thought it would be good fun to reduce this cocky youngster to size. Boxing is the one game where a man can be debunked more quickly, and more effectively, than in any other sport. The visitor was invited to strip and try his luck against one of the star pupils who outweighed him by nearly a stone. A few minutes later the debunking process was on its way. But as it turned out, the joke was very much against me, for in the next half-hour the newcomer had made good his threat, and flattened out all my three championship contenders, and smilingly inquired if I had anything else to offer him.

Subsequent inquiries revealed that this amazing youngster had run away from home when he was only fourteen years of age and had signed on as a stoker on a boat plying between England and Australia. He had never been taught the finer points of the game, but in the course of his work he frequently got mixed up in brawls with other stokers, and when that happened it was a question of the survival of the fittest. A hard school indeed. After his astonishing performance he was promptly enrolled as a private member. His success as an amateur was so phenomenal that within six months he was permitted to join the paid ranks and in his second professional appearance he won the South African feather-weight championship.

Billy Allen—for that was his name—successfully defended his title against all comers for a period of two years, and scored a knock-out each time his title was at stake. Among his victims was Clarence Walker, who had previously won a world title for South Africa at the Olympic Games. Walker was treated to a second knock-out in a return fight. Subsequently Allen toured Australia, where he had five fights and won them all by the knock-out. Weight for weight, Allen was undoubtedly the most terrific puncher ever produced in South African boxing, and whilst his hands lasted, no boxer ever went the distance with him. But if the boxing side of the enterprise produced a Billy Allen, the promoting side was instrumental in producing ' Professor Morrisey ', an even more astonishing character.

For my next promotion I had engaged Dave Meekin, the famous Australian middle-weight, who had previously lost on points to Jimmy Clabby over twenty rounds in a fight that was billed as being for the world's middle-weight title. Dave was not only a slick performer in the ring, but also a showman of the first order. On this occasion he had brought with him

' Professor Morrisey '—the world's greatest snake man. Morrisey was no professor from the point of view of educational attainments, but in his particular line of business he could leave any professor ' deep in the woods '. His personal appearance made the title of professor a ludicrous incongruity. He stood only 5 feet, weighed barely 100 lb., had three front teeth missing in his upper jaw, whilst around his neck he wore a red scarf, the ends of which were pulled through a massive gold ring which was studded with two large diamonds. In all the time I knew him I never saw him dressed in anything but an open khaki shirt, a pair of riding-breeches, and top boots. And never before, or since, has the English language been subjected to the kind of mauling it received from ' Professor ' Morrisey.

I was soon on terms of close friendship with the ' Professor ', and in the course of conversation he informed me that his act, apart from lecturing on the habits and poisons of snakes, consisted of taking the bites of the most poisonous reptiles known to man. He had brought with him an amazing collection of snakes and lizards—including the deadly King Cobra of India—a 12-foot specimen. The notable exceptions in his collection were the black and green mambas, which, he informed me, he was anxious to procure, as he wished to open his show by taking the bite from the black mamba—Africa's deadliest reptile.

During the short time I had known him I had frequently seen Morrisey handle the snakes in his collection with the greatest indifference and impunity; even the King Cobra was treated with scant respect. For all that, his wild talk about taking a bite from a mamba did not impress me very much, as I felt certain the snake would be carefully ' doctored ' before it was allowed to bite him.

I think I am right in saying that no man, or beast, has ever survived the bite of a mamba without immediate recourse to ligatures, cauterization of wounds, and injections of a powerful antivenene serum. And even under the most favourable conditions of treatment, survival is by no means certain. So potent is the venom of the mamba that a single drop injected into the vein of a jackal by means of a hypodermic needle proved fatal before the needle could be withdrawn. The mamba, with its speed, accuracy, aggressiveness, and the lethal quality of its venom, is the most feared reptile in all Africa, and in parts where it is frequently encountered it has been aptly named ' the shadow of death '. Morrisey was fully aware of all this, but he insisted that he would take a bite from any mamba, any time, anywhere. I remained sceptical and fearful of the result should he ever be foolish enough to put this mad idea into practice with an undoctored snake.

Since his arrival he had gone to a lot of trouble in his efforts to procure specimens of mambas, offering generous cash rewards to anyone who would assist him in procuring one, but all with no result. On approaching me on the subject one morning, I advised him to try the sugar plantations on the north coast of Natal, where green mambas were said to be plentiful.

He immediately fell in with my suggestion. The next instant he had hailed a ricksha-boy and insisted that I accompany him in order that we might investigate the possibilities of procuring a good specimen. Expecting the trip to be nothing more than a tour of inspection, I agreed, and a few minutes later we were on our way. The object of the trip was explained to the ricksha boy, who assured us he knew just where mambas were to be found. An hour or more later we came to a stop near a large plantation—we had arrived in Mambaland.

Inquiries from native labourers on the spot confirmed that there were plenty of mambas about, but they one and all turned a deaf ear to Morrisey's suggestion that they help him find one. His appeal to me to accompany him on his quest had a similar result, and finally Morrisey set out on his own. It was quite two hours later before we saw him again. This time he was not entirely alone, for in his right hand he proudly displayed a 7-feet green mamba which he had captured. He was highly excited and gave a graphic account of the trouble he had had to secure the trophy, and hastened to assure me that the snake had now settled down and was ' quite harmless '.

Only now did it begin to dawn on me that it was Morrisey's intention to take the mamba back to town with him, seated in a ricksha in which I would be a fellow passenger. The ricksha boy, by this time, was watching proceedings from a distance of 20 yards, and I also kept at a respectful distance.

My suggestion that he release the snake and return again later, better equipped to carry such deadly cargo, was turned down flat. Morrisey was determined to take his prize back with him, and I was equally determined to have no part in this mad escapade. In the end we compromised. The snake was pushed into his shirt, his belt and buttons were securely fastened and, for additional security, my tie was fastened round his neck below the collar, thus leaving no loophole for the reptile to escape. The ricksha boy's objections were overcome with the promise of a generous cash reward, and once again we were on our way.

I shall always look upon that ride back to town as one of the most nerve-wracking experiences of my life. Never for a moment did I permit my eyes to wander from the ominous bulge on Morrisey's waist-line. The richska boy was equally wary, and his attention was directed to Morrisey more often than to the road ahead of him. We finally got back to town shortly before sunset, and I lost no time in vacating that ricksha the moment it came to a stop. Morrisey, highly elated with the result of the trip, was now proudly exhibiting his prize to a number of onlookers who had gathered near his tent. For my part, I hurriedly quitted the scene, for fear I might be called upon for further assistance before the reptile was safely lodged in a cage.

I determined, however, to visit the show the following evening, it being the opening night, and Morrisey was busy announcing to all and sundry that he would, without fail, take a bite from the mamba at nine o'clock the next night. A poster notifying the public of this event was in the course of preparation when I left for home. On this trip Morrisey had amply proved his contention that even the most aggressive snake will only bite under provocation, or if it believes its safety is threatened. It is an intriguing point for those who are interested in snake psychology; the difficulty, of course, is to interpret the snake's thoughts correctly.

When I arrived on the scene the following evening at eight o'clock, the tent was already filling rapidly, and Dave was giving the public a streamlined sales talk in which he challenged Fitzsimmons, or any other snake authority in the world, to emulate the example of ' Professor ' Morrisey, who at nine o'clock sharp would take the bite of the mamba—the world's most poisonous reptile. Human nature being what it is, the tent was packed to suffocation long before 9 p.m. The spectators were turning out in force to see what a man looks like when death overtakes him as the result of a mamba bite.

All this time Morrisey was standing inside the snake enclosure, giving a long discourse on snakes, the action of their venom on human beings, their habits—no snake will ever attack without provocation, etc., etc. The mamba, meanwhile, was lying coiled up in the cage where it had been deposited the previous evening, to all intents and purposes fast asleep. At 9 p.m. a hush fell over the audience as Morrisey slowly walked to the cage and opened the door.

The mamba, however, remained motionless, and took no apparent interest in the proceedings until it was jabbed with a light stick. In an instant it shot through the open door with the speed of an arrow and landed in the centre of the enclosure, where it immediately reared up and adopted an aggressive pose, swinging its head from side to side, with fully one third of the anterior part of its body raised from the ground. So menacing was its attitude that an attack seemed imminent.

Although I had seen Morrisey handle the snake with complete disregard the previous day, watching the deadly reptile now, ready, and poised to strike, sent a chill down my spine. The audience was held spellbound for fully twenty seconds as Morrisey stood facing the swaying reptile, less than a foot away. Then, slowly, the mamba slid to the side of the enclosure, where it again started to coil up. A few seconds later the head was pressed down firmly to the ground with a forked stick and the snake was then lifted up and held aloft for the spectators to admire.

The stage was set for the final act.

Holding the snake firmly in his right hand, Morrisey roughly pushed his left forearm under its snout. As the fangs fastened on his arm he released his hold with the right hand, and for some seconds the mamba hung suspended in the air—fangs deeply embedded in the bare forearm. The jaws were then gently released and the snake replaced in its cage. After that Morrisey held out his arm for inspection. There was no doubt the bite was a full one, as blood started to flow from the puncture wounds. Morrisey then cauterised the wounds and poured some liquid into the incisions. He then thanked the audience for their patronage and expressed the hope to see them all back the following night, when he intended to take a bite from a puff-adder. Most of the onlookers must have felt dubious about seeing him again the next night, and remained in the vicinity to watch developments.

And well they might, for a few minutes later Morrisey slumped to the ground in a state of collapse. He was helped into a seat, where for a while he sat gasping for breath. I firmly believed that it was the beginning of the end, and suggested that a doctor be called without delay. The suggestion was immediately turned down, Morrisey claiming that he would soon be all right. By now he was showing all the signs of neurotoxic poisoning: troubled breathing, dilated eyes, rapid pulse and pains in the arm. We managed to get him to bed, where his condition seemed to deteriorate. I remained with him until midnight; he was then complaining of a feeling of suffocation and his sight was failing. When I left, a few minutes later, I felt convinced the end would not be long delayed.

At this time I had a great deal to do in connexion with the forthcoming promotion, and it was well after ten o'clock the next day before I was able to proceed to Morrisey's tent, where I expected to hear that he had died during the night. On entering the tent I was amazed to find him sitting at a table partaking of morning tea. He was still shaky, and showed unmistakable signs of the alarming experience of the previous night, and was loud in his denunciation of the mamba and the potency of its venom, the effects of which he did not shake off until after daybreak.

In spite of his definite assurance of the previous evening, Morrisey did not show for a further two days, when he made good his promise to take a bite from a puff-adder. The action of puff-adder poison is not as rapid as that of the mamba or cobra, and he showed no ill effects after the bite.

Despite his sensational success in withstanding the poison of the green mamba and puff-adder, Morrisey was still worrying about securing a black mamba, and in view of our first successful outing he now appealed to me to accompany him on a trip in search of one. The memory of that first expedition was still much too fresh in my mind to permit of another such adventure, and the invitation was promptly turned down.

A few days later I found him in a state of great excitement; he had at last succeeded in securing a good specimen of black mamba, from which he intended to take a bite that very night. I was present again on this occasion, and once more witnessed the gruesome spectacle of a deadly poisonous snake fastening its fangs into an accommodating victim. I did not stay to see the result, but it could not have been any worse than the previous occasion, for Morrisey was out and about as usual the following day. His incredible resistance to the venom of the most poisonous snakes in Africa puzzled not only the spectators, but also the medical profession. On one occasion three doctors visited his enclosure and accepted an invitation to examine the snake before it was allowed to bite him. They confirmed that the fangs and poison-ducts were intact. To satisfy sceptical onlookers one night, he allowed the mamba to bite a stray dog. The dog died within half an hour, and the exploit cost Morrisey £10 in the shape of a fine.

During the next week he took in turn the bites from mambas, cobras, and puff-adders—the two former neurotoxic, and the latter hæmotoxic, all deadly poisonous snakes.

Morrisey had utter faith in a serum which he claimed was infallible against all types of snake-poison; but as this serum was never injected, but simply poured into the wounds, it is doubtful whether it had such amazing neutralizing qualities. Moreover, he never resorted to ligatures after a bite—an absolute essential in the normal treatment of all snake-bites.

A more feasible explanation is that over many years Morrisey had systematically immunized himself against all types of snake-venom. The fact that his father and grandfather both followed the same profession may to some extent have provided him with a certain hereditary immunity. This immunity is, without doubt, bred among certain animals, such as the mongoose, meerkat, etc. The mongoose, weighing only 4 lb. or 5 lb., can absorb, and resist, far greater quantities of snake-venom than an elephant, weighing 4 or 5 tons. A big male elephant, bitten by a black mamba on the soft part of the trunk, collapsed in a little over an hour, and death supervened

D

in three hours.   It would be rare for a mongoose to succumb in such quick time.

Whatever the explanation in the case of Morrisey, the fact remains that no other man has ever wilfully subjected himself to the bites of any of the deadly species of African snakes, and least of all, the mamba.   That he subsequently died from the bite of a black mamba does not alter the fact that he could successfully resist the venom of the world's most poisonous snakes, for although I never saw him take the bite of the King Cobra, Morrisey assured me that he had often allowed this deadly reptile to inject a full dose of poison into him.

After I had got accustomed to Morrisey's gruesome performances in the enclosure, I witnessed some extremely amusing incidents when relationships between him and Dave became strained.   Morrisey had a distinct weakness for alcohol and he frequently indulged so freely that he was unable to perform.   When this happened there would be violent altercations between the two, and Dave would often be enraged to the point where he threatened physical violence.

Morrisey was in no way deterred by any threat coming from Dave.   On the contrary, he would immediately assume the role of aggressor, the vast difference in their statures notwithstanding.   When trouble loomed on the horizon, Morrisey took the timely precaution of pushing a poisonous snake into his shirt-front, from where it could be hauled out at a moment's notice.   Dave had a wholesome respect for Morrisey's snakes and never tempted fate too far.   In this he showed sound judgement, for Morrisey solemnly assured me that if ever that ' big brute ' tried to lay a hand on him, he would immediately resort to snake treatment.   ' We have both got our own professions—let him stick to his, and I'll stick to mine; in that way we will both keep healthy.'

But Morrisey did not keep healthy too long.   His indiscriminate indulgence in alcohol was soon to prove his undoing. One night, whilst under the influence, he dished out some rough treatment to a puff-adder.   The snake responded by driving one of its fangs deep into his thumb-nail.   In forcing the snake to release its grip, the fang was broken off deep down in the nail.   It was not until late the next afternoon that a doctor was called in to remove the broken piece of fang.   By that

time an acute inflammation had set in, and the thumb was
badly poisoned. This misfortune led to another wild bout of
drinking, and later that same night, Morrisey again took a
bite from a black mamba.

It proved to be the last bite he ever took, for after a few
minutes he collapsed outside his tent door, and later that night
he was taken to the Addington Hospital in Durban, where he
died ten days later. The combined effects of alcoholic and
snake-poison had proved too much for him in the end. Just
to what extent the mamba poison contributed to his death is
difficult to determine. Morrisey was certainly the first victim
to survive a fatal bite for ten days. But there we must be
guided by the hospital records, and they state that ' Professor '
Morrisey died ' as the result of a snake-bite '.

The Meekin–Oliver promotion unfortunately turned out to
be a financial flop, due to the fact that a tramway strike had
broken out some days before the date of the contest. The
promotion, however, is of historical interest to the boxing game
in South Africa. Previous to this, professional boxing had
been banned for twenty years in the Union, and it was as a
result of this contest, which I had advertised as a twenty-round
amateur bout for a 100-guinea trophy, that Mr. Thomas
Boydell, M.P., introduced, and had a Bill passed in Parliament,
legalizing professional boxing in South Africa. Since those
days South Africa has produced one world champion and
promoted at least three world title fights.

The heavy loss I sustained in this last promotion, and the
waning public interest in the game, decided me to go back to
Central Africa. My health was fully restored, and I had an
overwhelming longing to return to the bush and hunting.

It was at that time that I received a letter from a firm of
lawyers in Durban, asking me to call on them to discuss a
matter which they believed would be of ' considerable interest '
to me. I duly presented myself at their offices, to learn that
my paternal grandmother had died some two years earlier and
that I was a beneficiary under her will. It had taken them all
that time to discover my whereabouts and contact me. The
amount accruing to me from this will was not known at the
moment, but having established my identity, I could expect
full details in the near future. It was three weeks later when

I again presented myself at the lawyers' offices to learn that my share of the legacy amounted to exactly £2 12s. But for this unprofitable delay I should have been back in Central Africa at least three weeks earlier. A week later I was on my way to Jadotville in the Belgian Congo.

CHAPTER VI

EARLY CONGO DAYS

W HEN I LANDED in the Belgian Congo it was, for some reason or other, still referred to as 'the White Man's Grave'. During all the years I spent in that delightful country I never had reason to believe that it was any worse from climatic or health points of view than any other African territory. In fact it was much better than most, and in only one important respect did it differ from the others, and that was that in those days there was no extradition treaty in existence between the Congo and other territories. As a result, the country became an asylum for all sorts of undesirables and misfits from other parts.

But in spite of this collection of savoury and unsavoury characters, there was very little crime of a serious nature. The most persistent offenders were those who sought escape from boredom in the numerous bars and cafés in the towns. Liquor was cheaper, and wages higher, than anywhere else on the African continent, and drink provided most of the amusements—as also the tragedies.

Coming in to Elisabethville one morning, I passed a hand-cart with a coffin on board. This was a funeral procession which had then halted outside one of the pubs, where the mourners had gone to assuage their sorrow. Two days later I passed the same procession two streets farther down town. The mourners were then inside the last bar but one, on their way to the cemetery. On this occasion a sorrowing husband was taking his late wife to her last resting-place. As there was still one other bar to pass and a mile of road to travel before they would reach the cemetery, the procession probably did not reach their destination for another day or two.

This was typical of life in the Congo at that time. There was the case of the accountant who was serving a term of imprisonment for embezzlement. Prisoners serving a sentence in those days were allowed to have a bottle of beer with each meal; and the food was supplied from any hotel chosen by the convict. In the accountant's case the food from the hotels did not meet with his approval, and it was agreed that he should have his meals supplied by the gaoler. This arrangement proved satisfactory for all concerned until the gaoler's only daughter came in one day to announce that there was to be an increase in the family, a state of affairs for which the accountant was responsible. An offence of such a serious nature could not be condoned, and resulted in the offender being ' kicked out into the street ' without further ceremony.

I soon settled down in the copper-mining business, where I was employed as sampler. During the next two years I sampled every known ore in this vastly rich country. When the famous Chinkolobwe and Tantara uranium mines were about to go into production I was appointed chief sampler to these properties. Chinkolobwe then was, and perhaps still is today, the richest uranium mine in the world. Here, during the next six months, I gathered a most amazing collection of uranium specimens. When, some months later, the unauthorized possession of such specimens became illegal, it was with a view to getting my collection of several hundred pieces classified and legalized that I handed them in to the Geological Department.

A week or so later, when I called for my property, I was handed a small piece of pitch-blende ore with the accompanying permit. The rest of the collection was withheld, the chief geologist explaining that it was the finest collection of uranium specimens anywhere in the world. This collection is still in their Chituru Museum, and continues to be recognized as the finest in existence. It was so highly radio-active that shortly after it was placed in the general museum a new storage room had to be built for it.

At the time of my arrival in the Congo the Belgian franc still stood at a little over twenty-five to the pound sterling; and at that rate of exchange the average sterling earnings of employees was very high, but almost overnight the franc was devalued, and in a short time it stood at forty-five to the pound. The sterling value of the pay packet had thus dropped to nearly half its previous value. Like so many others then employed in the Congo, I had regular monthly commitments to meet in the south.

Things were getting worse every day, and I had just about reached an all-time low, when I hit on a brilliant idea to raise funds in a hurry. Two days later I inserted a challenge in the daily paper offering to meet any inhabitant in the Congo weighing up to 20 lb. more than myself, in a twenty-round contest on a winner-takes-the-lot basis. The challenge was not allowed to gather dust, and the next day I was signed up to meet Lavinsky, the recognized light-weight champion of the Congo, in a twenty-round contest at Elisabethville.

At the time I was domiciled in Jadotville—100 miles away—and did not make my appearance in Elisabethville until the day of the fight. At weighing-in time I found that my opponent had not only a weight advantage of 15 lb., but also an advantage in the betting of five to one. I was a stranger—an outsider—and nobody wanted to know anything about me, and everyone assured me I was in for the beating of my life. In the end I began to believe that a 60/40 or 70/30 division of the purse would have been a much better idea, but it was too late now to alter the arrangements. That night the hall was packed to suffocation, and when Lavinsky took the count in the fifth round I felt relieved to think that I had saved the pressing financial situation.

I was not so happy a few minutes later, when I learned that the booking of reserved seats had been entrusted to Lavinsky himself. Firmly convinced that the winning share of the purse would come to him anyway, he had set about spending what he believed was ' payment in advance '. All that was left for me was the cash taken at the doors that night—a little over £100. Thus, in spite of the ' winner-takes-the-lot ' agreement, it was the loser who netted 80 per cent of the spoils.

Some five years later, when defending the title for the last time, in the ' biggest-ever ' sporting event in the Congo, the result was a draw over fifteen rounds. My opponent and I stood to share more than £600. But sometime between the first and fifteenth round the promoters of that fight vanished from sight. In the ring I was too busy watching my opponent, and I am still waiting for my share of the spoils. My opponent on this occasion was a Swiss, who held an important position in one of the leading stores; the management took a bad view of the fact of his having appeared in a professional boxing match, and he was dismissed.   Losing his share of the purse as well as his employment must have proved too much for the poor fellow.   A few days later he was found dead in his apartment, having taken an overdose of sleeping draught.

In my occupation as sampler I moved freely all over the country, and there were many opportunities for hunting—in fact, it was hunting alone that could supply the necessary meat for large safaris, far out in the bush.   It was on one of these trips that I was accompanied by a Belgian friend who was also a keen hunter.   We were many miles beyond Kambove—one of the oldest copper-mines in the country, and we had pitched our camp at a spot where we expected to remain for at least a week.

Early on our first evening in camp trouble started with a prowling leopard, the attraction being a mongrel dog which my friend had brought along.   About midnight there was a violent disturbance quite close to us, and from the yelping of the dog it was clear that it had fallen victim to the leopard. By the time we were able to investigate the trouble with a torch both leopard and dog had vanished.

My friend was incensed at the loss of his dog, and early next morning he insisted that we should go in search of the prowler. I tried to dissuade him, but in spite of my objections we were soon on the trail, which shortly led into dense, close bush, and grass.   In this kind of country a leopard can be extremely dangerous, and I again tried to persuade my friend to abandon the trail and wait for the leopard to put in an appearance that night, but he was determined to follow the marauder and settle the score there and then.

For a time we stuck to the trail together, but after a while we became separated, each following a different direction.   A few minutes later a shot rang out quite close to me, and this was followed almost immediately by loud screams.   I rushed at once to the spot from which the screaming came, but when I arrived on the scene it was already too late.   By that time my friend was lying on the ground and the leopard was giving him a savage mauling.   On seeing me she turned from him, and was actually drawing back her ears, ready for the charge, when I placed a bullet between her eyes.

A quick glance at my friend made it obvious that he was

beyond all help. He did not remain conscious long enough to give me a full account of what had happened, but it was not difficult to reconstruct the tragedy. Quite close to where he lay were two leopard cubs inside an ant-bear hole, at the mouth of which was the carcass of the dog. The mother must have been on the look-out when my friend walked into this hornet's nest, and this brought forth an immediate charge. The shot he had fired was badly placed, and only aggravated matters. Before he could fire a second shot the infuriated beast was on top of him, and in a few seconds he was almost completely disembowelled, and his throat and face were badly lacerated as the result of the vicious attack with both fangs and claws. Weight for weight, the leopard is, to my mind, the most deadly killer of all, and will attack on the slightest provocation. My friend did not long survive the mauling he had received. In less than an hour it was all over.

I collected the two cubs, one of which died shortly after; the other grew into a magnificent specimen, and I kept him as a pet for more than five years. He was the first of many others I reared as pets during the next twenty years. Well managed, they grow into delightful pets, and give no trouble at all. In the end I became so fond of the spotted cats that I never troubled to kill them on the many occasions I came across them in the bush.

Unmolested in its natural state, the leopard is completely harmless where human beings are concerned. I have yet to hear of an instance where a leopard has turned man-eater, or gone out of its way to interfere with man without provocation. But once he is provoked, it is only a bullet in the right spot that will break down the charge. Given the right conditions, he can be equally as dangerous as any lion. This applies especially in the case of a female fighting to protect its young. Hundreds of lion cubs have been collected all over Africa after they have been abandoned by their parents in face of danger. The only way a leopard cub can be collected in similar circumstances would be over its dead mother's body.

Some time after this leopard adventure I was to share in another tragedy. On this occasion I was hunting elephant in the Lualaba country with a friend named Booysen. The country was well stocked with elephants, but worth-while tuskers were by no means plentiful. Early one morning Booysen and I left camp hunting in opposite directions. Later, during the course of the morning, I passed a big herd of elephants in which there were several cows and calves, and a few young bulls, but no tusker of any account. The herd were grazing out in a general direction towards our camp, and I gave them no further thought.

It was just before sunset when I got back to camp, to find the place in an uproar. Booysen had had a blank day and returned to camp shortly after noon. An hour or so later the herd I had encountered earlier in the day passed close to his tent. They were well scattered, and some minutes after they had passed, a very young calf which was lagging a long way behind came right up to the spot where Booysen was sitting. The temptation must have proved too great for him, and he at once got hold of the calf and hung on for all he was worth.

Thoroughly startled by this unexpected rough handling, the calf set up a loud squeal, and Booysen was still struggling to hold it down when the mother suddenly appeared. She immediately gathered him up in her trunk and dashed him to the ground. The performance was repeated several times, and after satisfying herself that Booysen was dead, she proceeded to roll over the corpse.

I arrived on the scene fully two hours later. By that time the herd had already departed, and there was nothing left for me to do but collect what remained of my friend—a pulp of mangled flesh. In my experience with elephants I have not found them to be vindictive killers, but in the case of a mother fighting for the protection of her young there is no limit to her vindictiveness. For an experienced hunter, such as he was, Booysen was guilty of an inexplicable folly, and he paid heavily for his lapse.

At this time accidents in the field seemed to follow in rapid succession, for it was not long after the elephant incident that I was again out in the Lualaba country. On this occasion I was accompanied by a brother of the Booysen who had come to such a tragic end with the elephant. At one stage of our hunting we set up different camps a few miles apart.

Early one morning a native runner came to my camp to report that Booysen had been badly mauled by a wounded lion. I immediately proceeded to his camp, where he had been carried by his natives after the accident. The trouble this time was once more due to carelessness. Booysen was a crack shot and, like his brother, a very experienced hunter. But this did not prevent him from following a badly wounded lion into close country. The lion had attacked unexpectedly, and gave him a tremendous mauling before a gun-bearer came to the rescue and shot the brute. By that time Booysen had suffered such serious injuries that an arm and leg had subsequently to be amputated, the wounds having turned septic, and it was more than two years later before he was finally discharged from hospital in Elisabethville—a permanent cripple.

If there was any luck in this episode, it was the fact that Booysen had fractured the lower jaw of the lion with his shot, and this prevented the beast from using its fangs to full advantage. Booysen's account of the lion lying on top of him, making frantic efforts to use its deadly fangs, was one of the most blood-curdling hunting stories I ever listened to. One needs very little imagination to picture the ordeal he must have gone through before the gun-bearer came to his rescue.

These two Booysen brothers were, as already stated, both experienced hunters, and excellent shots to boot, but, like so many other hunters, they grew careless and took unnecessary risks. On the trail of the dangerous animals in Africa the first liberty one takes is generally the last. With the exception of the eland, I know of no animal that will fail to fight back when it is cornered, and this is especially true in the case of wounded animals. Once an animal is badly wounded its main desire is to escape as quickly and effectively as possible from further injury, and with the exception of the buffalo, who will resort to strategy in order to retaliate, I do not believe that any other animal ever resorts to cunning for this purpose. In the case of elephant, rhino, lion, and such recognized dangerous animals, they will strive to get as far away as possible from their pursuer and find a place to hide.

In following the trail of a wounded animal a good deal of time is often lost, and during that time the animal stiffens up so much that it is reluctant to move. If in such circumstances it is approached too closely, it will prefer attack to flight. This has nothing to do with cunning or vindictiveness. With the buffalo it is quite a different story, and there is no serious hunter in Africa who is not aware of the danger of an ambush and charge from behind should the trail be lost.

I once had an opportunity to watch a wounded bull going into ambush and doubling back on its track.   The details are worth relating.   When on the Lualaba River in the Belgian Congo one morning we spotted a big bull lying under a tree. The range was well over 300 yards, but the bull had scented us and was about to take off when I took a snap shot at it.   I could hear the bullet strike, and from the spasmodic jump he made, I knew that the shot was well placed in the chest.   The bull set off at a fast pace, and I immediately ran for a tree, which I mounted, and from which I could watch proceedings. He was quite unaware of my whereabouts, but I could watch the movements of the trackers who were following in the direction he had run.

For a distance of about 200 yards from where he had stopped the bullet was open country with short grass.   Farther ahead was a cluster of dense, high grass, about 70 yards long, and for this cluster he was making at a rapid pace.   On two occasions he stopped deliberately and looked back; apparently satisfied that he was being followed, he resumed his course towards the long grass until he reached its near end.   Now he deliberately turned off to the left, and kept moving forward until he had reached the far end of the cluster.   Here he stopped again and looked back in the direction where he had last seen the natives following him.   Satisfied that they were still on his trail, he suddenly entered the long grass at the extreme end, and from there he rapidly doubled back until he had reached a point quite close to the near end of the tall grass.   One more look to make sure he was still being followed, and he went down in a prone position.

At short intervals he raised his head slowly and looked intently in the direction from which the natives were coming. This performance was repeated on at least three occasions. By now the natives had approached to within 200 yards of him; to their left, and within easy range, were some tall trees which they could easily mount in time in case of trouble.   But at this point I signalled for them to stop.   Again the bull lifted his head slowly; it was quite obvious that he could see the natives standing in a group. At this stage he must have realized that they scented danger. It is rare for a buffalo to charge from such a long distance, but this brute had made up his mind that it was time to go into action, or lose the opportunity of getting to grips with his pursuers. Now there was a twitching of the tail, a swinging of the head, and slowly he was rising to his knees. It was quite obvious that in the next instant he would come out in full charge. Meanwhile I had been watching his every movement from the tree, and had kept him well aligned in my sights. Another vicious swing of the head and a loud grunt, and he was ready to take off. It was at that moment that I brought proceedings to a close with a heavy .404 slug in the neck. This bull was well aware of the fact that he was being trailed, and in striking out to the left of the patch of long grass, his intention was to lead the natives on a trail which he made sure of covering by doubling back unseen. But for the fact that, unknown to him, I was watching proceedings, and was able to signal to the trackers, there would have been one more buffalo accident to record.

However, on following the trail of a wounded beast, the hunter has not always the advantage of a tree and open country from which to make observations, and once the animal has entered close country or long grass, even the best trackers cannot tell what awaits them ahead. Every trail inevitably leads to where the quarry lies waiting and watching further developments until death overtakes it. In such cases a policy of patience is by far the best, and whenever I have been doubtful, especially in the case of buffalo, I have preferred to wait for the vultures to give the lead. Their uncanny eyesight soon brings them to the spot where a badly wounded animal has taken cover. As long as they sit and watch from branches nearby it is certain that danger lies ahead, and to approach such a spot heedlessly is the height of folly. A dead hunter can do nothing to alleviate the suffering of a wounded animal.

By the time I returned from this last ill-fated safari I had completed six years in the Congo, and my second long leave in Europe was due. The first overseas leave had been sacrificed to the uranium job which I have mentioned earlier. I was only a few days before I was due to set off for Brussels that the management persuaded me once again to cancel my leave.

On this occasion in order to take over the catering contract for their various messes and restaurants in Jadotville. My knowledge of catering at the time was extremely limited, and the only reason I was offered the contract was because it was felt that, in view of my boxing and jiu-jitsu experience, I would be able to control the unruly elements among the employees. The previous concessionaire was at the moment lying in hospital with three fractured ribs—the result of a difference of opinion with one of the customers. It was a contract with unlimited financial prospects, but it also entailed the greatest difficulties in keeping the customers subdued. The vast construction programme then in progress had brought out some of the most unsavoury characters from Belgium, and free fights with knives, bottles, and sticks were the order of the day.

After serious consideration I decided to accept the proposition on a six-months-trial basis. Those first six months taxed my resources to the extreme limit, but I managed to see the period through with only one major upset which led to a spot of violence. That was when the camp bully showed up one night, mounted the counter, and with two broken bottles in his hands, offered to match himself against anyone in the place. A few minutes later we loaded him into a wheelbarrow and sent him off to hospital with a dislocated shoulder and slight concussion. After that I found it much easier to reason with the unruly elements, and at the end of the six months the contract was extended to take in all the properties in the Congo for an indefinite period. For the next nine years I filled the role of chief caterer in the Belgian Congo. During this period I developed an important importing business, several agencies, printing works, etc., etc. The business proved a great success from the beginning, and I was now making money on a scale I had never dreamt of before.

At the end of nine years I decided that I had saved enough to retire and settle down in Europe. The business was disposed of and I booked passage for Belgium. It was just at that time that the Talkie Cinemas were making their appearance in Europe and South Africa. A week later my passage to Europe was cancelled, and I entered the show business with cinemas in Elisabethville and Jadotville, with others under construction in the interior. I firmly believed that I was on the road that would lead to another fortune. In actual fact I had entered a road that was to lead to utter disaster. The terrific slump in the price of copper in the early 'thirties soon brought the Congo to a complete standstill, and it took exactly two years for a million and a half francs to go down the drain. The Congo had reached bedrock financially, and the future was as dark as could be imagined.

CHAPTER VII

ON THE LUPA GOLDFIELD

DURING THE COURSE of the past month, January 1956, the price of copper rose to £417 on the London Metal Exchange. This was an all-time high figure for this commodity, and in spite of this elevated price, the demand still exceeded the supply. In 1932 the other extreme was reached, and the price of copper fell to £28 per ton, and even at that low price supplies far exceeded the demand and there was a glut on the market. Producers all over the world faced the most serious crisis in the history of copper, and many of them verged on the border of extinction. In due course the world's leading producers met in New York and there a quota system was inaugurated.

The Belgian Congo, where I was then domiciled, was one of the countries most seriously affected by this new arrangement, for as a result of the long period of stagnation the amount of copper they had amassed on surface exceeded by far the amount they were permitted to sell during the next two years. In a short time the production side of the industry was at a complete standstill and the Congo found itself in the midst of a general exodus. Each week saw trainloads of workers on their way back to Belgium, and commercial life became completely disrupted. When the exodus was at its height it was a daily occurrence to see families, booked to return to Europe, hold public auctions of their possessions, and it was rare indeed for a well-furnished house to realize more than £2; the only buyers were the natives from the various compounds. A friend of mine who had tried for the best part of a month to dispose of a late model Ford Coupe still had found no buyer for it an hour before his train was due to depart. The car was finally enchanged for a vest-pocket camera, and the new owner complained volubly that he had been swindled when he found there was not sufficient petrol in the tank to take him back home.

This wholesale repatriation of employees affected not only

the men who were brought out from Europe on contracts, but also the locally engaged workers, for they were retrenched and paid off without any provision for their repatriation. The population rapidly dwindled away, and those who were unable to finance their way out of the Congo were fed at Government expense in the numerous soup kitchens which had been opened for the purpose throughout the country.

The successful cinema business I had opened previously was the first to suffer under the changed conditions. When people cannot afford to buy their daily food there is not much to spend on entertainments. But the problem of diminished audiences was not the only one with which I was faced. I had previously entered into an agreement with all the leading producers to supply me weekly programmes for a period of five years. Programmes were all on long location, and extremely costly. It often happened that an evening session numbered only five customers. Frequently a programme would be shown for the benefit of a few friends whom I had invited, and more often programmes were returned to Europe unopened. This state of affairs continued for fully two years, and at the end of that time I was forced to close down. A project which under normal conditions should have established me in business permanently and brought me another fortune, had swallowed all my savings of the previous twelve years.

Like so many others, I was compelled to look for fresh pastures. It was at this time that news started to trickle through from the new Lupa Goldfield in Tanganyika Territory. Here, reports had it, men came in wheelbarrows and drove away in Rolls Royces. In my own case, it was a question of ' any port in a storm ', and ere long I was on my way to the new Eldorado in the capacity of accredited representative of the Essor group of newspapers in the Congo and Belgium. I was to report back to the Congo on conditions on the Lupa and at the same time I would exploit the conditions and prospects on the field on my own account.

Early one morning in February my five-ton truck was fully loaded and I was all set for the 1,000-mile journey to the Lupa Goldfield. My departure was preceded by numerous farewells and fêtes, for during my fifteen years' stay in the Congo I had mixed freely with all sections of the community. My activities

E

in the catering business, the inauguration of the cinemas, the formation of numerous sporting clubs, the organizing of many outstanding sporting events between athletes from the Rhodesias and South Africa against local talent, the many valuable trophies I had presented for competition, and my own participation in international boxing matches, had brought me many friends, and my departure now from the scene of so much happiness caused me a great deal of sadness. It was the end of yet another trail—a trail crowded with many memories.

The month of February is noted for its heavy seasonal rains, and road travel at this time of the year can be extremely hazardous. It happened frequently that the day's progress amounted to less than 3 miles. The road was, for the most part, a quagmire, and the truck would often sink axle deep into the mud, from where it had to be extricated under the greatest of difficulties, often in pouring rain. A few yards farther on the same performance would have to be repeated. When finally I reached Mbeya in Tanganyika Territory, I had been on the road for fully a month. An unpleasant feature of the trip was the numerous encounters with stragglers returning from the Lupa Goldfield. Their stories made unpleasant listening, for none of these stragglers had done any good on the Lupa, and if they entered the field on wheelbarrows, they were now walking out on their flat feet. The general opinion I gathered from this community, was that if one was *lucky* one might strike it rich, but in general, for every one digger who struck it rich on the Lupa there were ten who slowly starved to death.

Arrived at Mbeya, which is 35 miles from the goldfield, I immediately started making inquiries as to the true conditions on the field. I gathered that there were then some 1,100 diggers operating in the area. By far the greater majority were in a bad way, and found it difficult to make ends meet. There was a middle class who managed to pay their way and live reasonably well; a small number was doing very well. Hardly a week passed without some digger or other making a rich strike. If one remained on the field long enough and tried hard enough, there was a reasonable chance of making good in the end. What I was listening to was the unvarnished truth of the story of every alluvial goldfield in history. It was nothing strange, but it all sounded very nebulous, and the uncertainty in the matter of the time factor before one ' struck it rich ' was somewhat disconcerting.

The information I had gathered so far was based mainly on general opinions; official data, I was informed, would be obtainable at the Mines Department at Chunya, together with all the necessary statistics of the field. Chunya was a little mining village, without hotel, post office, hospital, bank, school, or any other public facility. The Mines Department functioned only for the purpose of issuing licences, settling the numerous disputes in the matter of irregular pegging, collecting, and checking returns from the diggers on the field.

Two days later I presented myself at the Mines Office in my accredited capacity of newspaper representative. After considerable haggling, the statistics of the field were made available to me, and after an hour's study it was only the thought of another 1,000-mile journey over rain-sodden roads and mud marshes that prevented me from returning immediately to the Congo.

From the figures placed at my disposal it appeared that actually there were 1,020 diggers operating on the field at that moment. The average monthly recovery of a digger amounted to £7 10s. Diggers were not allowed to operate with less than ten natives per claim. Native wages averaged 8s. per month and food 5s. On this basis of calculation, the average digger was left with the princely sum of 20s. per month with which to pay for his food and living and tools and equipment. There were many married men on the field, and there were several diggers who rarely made less than £100 net profit per month —reducing to that extent the monthly average of those who were less fortunate. These figures were staggering indeed, and it remained now to examine the conditions under which the average digger toiled and lived on this new Eldorado in Tanganyika Territory.

Whilst I was busy preparing statistics in the Mines Office at Chunya, a report came in that there had been a big strike at Kungutas, a mining camp 15 miles away. By then I had secured my prospecting permit and claim licences. A day or two later I was on my way to Kungutas to try my luck and to study at first hand what effects a big strike had on the digging community. I had by this time engaged a native headman with thirty labourers, whom I had equipped with the necessary tools, which consisted mainly of alluvial pans, picks, shovels, hammers, and drills. There was never a shortage of native labour on the Lupa. Like the Europeans for whom they worked, the native population depended mainly on luck, and were always prepared to share with their masters the rigours and fortunes of the field, hoping that some time, sooner or later, the Goddess of Fortune would relent and lead them to the longed-for ' lucky strike '.

Most of these natives were expert panners and prospectors, but they were also the most infamous liars and thieves I ever encountered anywhere. No native ever applied to me for work without assuring me that he knew of a place where there was plenty of gold. As often as not the statement would be supported by a practical demonstration—a piece of gold, usually stolen from a previous employer—and an assurance that there was plenty more where that piece came from. Generally one had to dig down several feet in hard clay to get to the ' wash ' in the river-beds where the gold is located, and many thousands of pits have been dug in barren ground on the Lupa on assurances from native diggers. If a prospect paid off, the native would come for his reward; if the prospect turned out a failure—which it generally did—it was ' *shauri ya Mungu* ' (the will of God), and the unfortunate digger would have to try somewhere else.

When I arrived at Kungutas I found all the indications of a feverish ' rush '. Tents and shacks were being erected all over an area of some 4 square miles. Although a bond of sympathy existed between diggers on the field, it never extended to the point where they would divulge any secrets or give away any information in the event of a strike. On the advice of my native headman, I forthwith staked two claims and immediately started digging operations. At the end of ten days my labour force was still working at top speed, but had failed to discover as much as a trace of gold. On inquiring from other diggers in the vicinity how they were faring, I found that for the greater part their fortunes were on a par with my own—hope by the ton but gold conspicuous by its absence.

Where diggers congregate as the result of news of a strike, conditions soon become intolerable. In the present case the nearest drinking-water was 6 miles away; firewood was to all intents and purposes unprocurable; vegetables, fresh meat, or bread were unobtainable, and the small supplies that filtered through were eagerly snapped up by those who were lucky enough to be in the vicinity when such supplies arrived on the scene.

At this time there were some 200 diggers congregated at Kungutas. At a conservative estimate each digger employed the minimum ten natives prescribed by law. In addition there were the usual hangers on—women, children, and the vultures whose speciality was illicit gold-buying: the curse of every alluvial goldfield. When there is a rush for gold, no digger will ever dream of diverting labour for the purpose of preparing sanitary conveniences, however simple.

At Kungutas conditions rapidly deteriorated, and soon became unbearable from any human standpoint. In a short time there was a serious outbreak of dysentery in the camp, and this was soon followed by an epidemic of typhoid. Scurvy was rampart among the native labourers, and ere long many Europeans were similarly afflicted. On the entire field there was only one doctor, who was interested in gold, and not in medicine. If one fell ill within reasonable distance of the doctor there was a fair chance of receiving medical advice— I use the word advisedly, for the doctor's equipment consisted mainly of picks and pans and shovels. In this respect one could hardly blame him, for it was only on the rarest occasions that a digger was ever possessed of the means, or the conscience, to pay for medical treatment.

I remained at Kungutas for another fortnight. At the end of that time I had not found a trace of gold, and I decided to pack up. By then many others had taken a similar decision, and there was a general exodus from the Kungutas area. I subsequently discovered that the lucky strike which caused the rush to Kungutas was not alluvial, but illuvial—in other words, the gold was not scattered, as happens in the case of alluvial deposits, but adhered to an eroded or oxidized reef. The only gold ever found in this particular area was taken from the small reef which the original discoverer had found and pegged. The other 199 diggers, including myself and some 2,500 natives, were the victims of another end-of-the-rainbow chase.

Kungutas was my first attempt at alluvial, and the result was distinctly disheartening. I had come here to investigate the possibilities of the field, and I decided not to tempt fortune any further until I had a better working knowledge of alluvial mining and the general conditions. From the Mines Department I obtained a map and information as to the most promising centres, and to these places I now proceeded to gather more information and experience. In turn I visited all the likely areas and spent some time in each.

The lure of gold is something no one has ever been able to fathom. In each of the places I visited I found conditions very similar to those which obtained at the famous Kungutas rush. There were several diggers doing quite well, but wherever I went I saw poverty and misery such as I had never seen before. A great many existed on the eternal diet of maize-meal and dry beans. In this respect they did not differ from the natives. This pertained all over the Lower Lupa. On the Upper Lupa, I was informed, there was a small colony of immigrants from the Congo who had preceded me and were doing very well. I decided to visit this area, where I encountered an old friend from the Congo. In reply to my inquiry about his progress, he informed me that he was not doing too badly. ' You see, my friend,' he said, ' until yesterday I was living on beans and buffalo meat, but now I have no more money to buy beans. Fortunately I brought a good supply of ammunition with me, and until the weather breaks it will have to be buffalo without the beans.' Soon after this interview my friend, who was an Italian, decided that the conditions on the Lupa were too tough for him, and enlisted in the Italian army in Abyssinia. There he was fated to strike something a good deal tougher than the Lupa goldfield, for he was captured early in the war by an Abyssinian patrol and subjected to the unspeakable brutality these savages reserved for prisoners of war.

In a short time I managed to traverse the entire field, and by and large the story was always the same : hardship and misery for many, with but an occasional lucky strike by a lucky individual. But in spite of the appalling conditions prevailing on the field, it was only on rare occasions that I met a digger who was anxious to exchange his vocation for more stable employment. In all but a very few cases the lure of gold had entered deeply into their souls and paralysed their reasoning powers.

After I had completed my tour of the Upper Lupa I felt that my mission of inquiry was at an end, and I sent in fully detailed reports to the Essor, and then sat down to take stock of my own position. In view of the information I had gathered and my disastrous experiences in the alluvial digging business, I decided to return to the Congo. However bad conditions were there, the human touch still remained. On the Lupa goldfield the human touch had long since been lost— if it ever existed. Life was bestial, degrading, and offered no security whatever. The occasional *lucky strike* was much too isolated and rare to make the proposition attractive in any way. The lure of gold had not yet gripped me, as it had so many others, and I decided to get out before I drifted too far.

One morning, whilst I was busy putting the final touches to my truck and preparing for the return journey, a native messenger brought me a letter from the managing director of an important mining group which was soon to start reef-mining in the Lupa area. The writer suggested that I should call on him to discuss a business matter which might prove of interest to me. That letter was instrumental in delaying my departure from the Lupa for another fifteen years. The director in question had met me earlier in the Belgian Congo and knew about my catering activities there. He was anxious that I should accept a similar contract with their group. They expected to start active mining operations within six months, by which time they would have a minimum of 250 employees on the property. The terms were similar to those under which I had previously operated in the Congo, and I resolved to accept the offer.

During the time I was waiting for the contract to come into effect I decided I would give alluvial a further trial, and once more I was back on the field. Again a gang of labourers was engaged, and I listened to the old story about gold being plentiful at a spot which was known only to my informant. The usual nugget of gold was once again in evidence, and on this occasion exceeded 2 oz. in weight. I promptly took possession of the nugget and informed the owner that if his story was true he would be suitably rewarded; if not, the gold would be sold to defray expenses. To this he readily agreed, and early the next morning we were on our way to yet another Eldorado.

The new claim was situated in the Maperi area, some 8 miles from my camp, and had not been prospected previously. The two following days were devoted to stripping overburden, and on the third day panning operations commenced. By eleven o'clock the panners had handed me over 5 oz. of gold, and when work ceased at four o'clock I had recovered over 15 oz. of gold and felt convinced that I was on the verge of a big discovery. The natives were wildly excited, as, with the bonus system then in existence, many of them had earned more in that one day than they would normally earn in a month. At daybreak the next morning we were all back on the claim. The results, however, were not nearly as good as on the previous day, and the recovery for the day was a little over 2 oz.

By the end of that week the vanguard of another rush began to appear. News of a strike travels rapidly on the field, and the news had got abroad that I was 'on gold'. Alas, it turned out to be another fruitless chase, for, apart from the two claims I had pegged, the Maperi area never paid dividends. Very few of those who had rushed to the spot were lucky enough to cover expenses, and my total for that month amounted to 45 oz. During the next month the recovery dropped daily, and my total takings for the month amounted to only 5 oz. The indications were that the claim had 'gone dry'. Next day I pulled up my pegs and once again I was on my way to pastures new.

At Maperi, in view of the successful start, I had contracted an unhealthy dose of gold fever; I felt convinced that it would be only a matter of time before I too would strike it rich. The conviction was strengthened when I heard later that my claims were re-pegged immediately after I had withdrawn, and the new owner had recovered 300 oz. during the first month. Five years later these Maperi claims were still being worked, and by that time they had yielded over 2,000 oz. of gold. It was a unique formation which I did not understand, and the gold was located at extreme depth. The true deposit was only a few feet below where I had left off, and was confined to a small area. Like so many other centres on the field, Maperi helped to write one more chapter in ' blood, sweat and tears ' .

After my experience at Maperi I took to a roving life on the field, trying my luck wherever I thought gold might be located. Even at this early stage I felt that the panning methods employed on the field were far too primitive, and that some sort of mechanization would prove more profitable and save time both in prospecting and working claims. Apart from a few sluice-boxes which could be used only in running water in river-beds, the entire field depended on native panners—a slow process, as a first-class panner rarely managed more than fifty pans in one day, and gold was often lost and stolen in the process.

I discussed the possibilities of more practical methods with many of the old hands, but none seemed very interested. They were, for the greater part, content with the existing methods. It was a free-and-easy life from the point of view of actual work, which consisted mainly of weighing the gold which the panners had recovered during the day. A good deal of the misery on the Lupa, I am convinced, was due to the indolence of the diggers themselves. All responsibilities were laid on the shoulders of the panner, whose duty it was to bring in sufficient gold to keep his master alive and provide his own wages. If the gold was not forthcoming it was just too bad— there would be no pay and no food for master or servant.

This irresponsible outlook was to a large extent encouraged by the Labour Office, which was very tolerant with pay defaulters. If a man was unlucky today, he may be lucky tomorrow and discharge his obligations. Natives were at all times prepared to accept I.O.U.'s in lieu of cash, and would keep a careful watch on a defaulter's activities. The moment he struck gold they would return and present their I.O.U.'s for payment, and as often as not they would join forces again in an endeavour to help recover the maximum amount of gold in the quickest possible time. It was a typical digger's life, and no one seemed unduly worried when things went bad, ' tomorrow is always another day and gold is just where you find it,' was the general philosophy of the field.

During the next few months I kept myself fully occupied digging for gold, with varying fortunes, and at the same time meeting some of the strangest characters imaginable. There was ' Doc ', an Irishman, and the best tropical diseases doctor I know of. At the time of my arrival near his camp he had three black-water patients on his hands; they were extremely bad cases and the prospects of pulling them through seemed very remote to me. Black-water fever is one of the most deadly of all tropical diseases, and is brought on by prolonged doses of malaria fever. The moment a man discovers that he is afflicted with black-water, he lies down, no matter where he finds himself. If it is in the bush, his blankets are brought out to him and a shelter is constructed over him, and there he remains until he is cured or dies. Movement of any sort is fatal in most cases. In the many years I spent in the Congo I saw hundreds of victims carried off by this deadly disease, and the chances of surviving a bad attack were never rated higher than 1 per cent. In ' Doc's ' cases all three patients were effectively cured without any subsequent ill effects.

In spite of his undoubted ability, ' Doc's ' activities in the medical profession were regulated strictly by events in the alluvial field. If gold was plentiful and needed his presence, it was well-nigh impossible to persuade him to attend to a case. When these conditions prevailed, patients had to find their way to his camp for attention, for he would in no circumstances leave his claims to the care of native workers. ' Doc ' was also a firm believer in alcoholic stimulants, and even when a patient was brought to his camp he would prove extremely difficult and contrary.

On the two occasions I appealed to him for help I fared so badly that I firmly resolved to dispense with his services entirely. The first occasion was when I contracted a bad dose of malaria. ' Doc ' was ' on gold ', and I had to be carried to his camp, 8 miles away. When I arrived it was sundowner time and he was busy entertaining friends Sundowner time with ' Doc ' generally started at 2 p.m. and often carried on until six o'clock next morning. On my arrival I explained what my trouble was, and begged him to give me an anti-malarial injection. ' Doc ' was very sympathetic and had me placed on a camp bed, promising to give me an injection as soon as he had finished his sundowner. Two hours later I was still lying in the same position, and ' Doc ' was then busy pouring his eighth sundowner.

By this time I felt so ill I did not care whether I ever received the injection or not. It must have been fully an hour later that I suddenly felt a needle being pushed into my buttocks. ' Doc ' had suddenly remembered the injection and promptly pushed a syringe through my trousers and shirt. It must have been the look of surprise on my face that prompted him to say, ' This is how we do it on the Lupa, my boy—you'll be a lot better in the morning.' All that night I shivered and tossed in a high fever, but the assault with the syringe had marked the end of his sympathy and interest; ' Doc ' was back on his sundowners. At the rate ' Doc ' was administering injections I estimated it would take fully three weeks to give me the requisite five injections. Early next morning I got my natives to carry me back to camp, where, with regular doses of quinine, I eventually effected my own cure.

The next time I had occasion to appeal to ' Doc ' for help was after I had suffered a maddening toothache for more than a week. By then my nerves were completely shattered and the pain made it impossible to sleep or rest. My previous experience with ' Doc ' had left me with the gravest of doubts as to the advisability of another appeal to him for help, but there was no alternative, and once more I presented myself at his camp. As I expected, it was sundowner time again when I arrived there. Doc was very sympathetic, but he made it clear that he was no dentist, and that before he could undertake the job it would be necessary for him to have a couple of sundowners in order to steady his nerves.

An hour later his nerves were steady enough to commence operations. The forceps were carefully placed over the affected tooth and I thanked heaven that I would soon be rid of the offending molar and the pain. The next instant there was a sickening cracking of bone in my jaw. Doc definitely was no dentist, and his nerves were far too steady. He had applied too much pressure, and the tooth was broken off deep in my gum. The pain was such that I kept running round the room in circles. Suddenly I heard ' Doc ' shouting for the cook to bring chloroform. I was suffering too much pain to interpret the meaning of it all, but now the cook-boy suddenly appeared with a tray containing a bottle of chloroform, cotton wool, and dressings.

It was quite clear that ' Doc ' was going to put me under in order to extract the other half of my tooth. He explained that to try to remove it without chloroform would cause me too much pain, and assured me that the cook was an old hand at the game and had often helped him to administer anæsthetics. It all sounded very plausible, and I had no doubt that ' this was the way we do it on the Lupa '. But I was not at all impressed, and I ultimately persuaded him to hand me the forceps and leave me to do the rest myself. I have not the power of description to tell adequately what I went through during that next hour, but at the end of that time I had managed to extract the last piece of bone from my jaw. Doc was very sincere in his expression of sympathy and immediately invited me to join him in a sundowner. When I left him I had accounted for the best part of his bottle, but I was still suffering a maddening pain. It was not long after this incident that, in spite of his great ability to heal other sufferers from tropical diseases of a deadly nature, ' Doc ' himself suffered an attack of typhoid fever and failed to minister successfully for himself, for he died on his lonely claim, miles out in the bush, almost unattended, a fortnight later.

This incident reminds me of another occasion some years later when the Lupa had become more civilized and there were now two doctors operating on the field. Again I was suffering from toothache and sent for a doctor. I told him the story of my previous experience and mentioned that I felt rather nervous in the circumstances. After some discussion it was decided that I be put under with an injection of Eva Pan, which would send me into a peaceful sleep whilst the tooth was extracted. I was duly put to sleep, and when I awoke the doctor had already departed, but on a chair in front of my bed lay the offending tooth. The toothache, however, was as violent as ever, and on closer examination I discovered that I had been deprived of a perfectly sound tooth, whilst the cause of the trouble was still firmly embedded in my jaw. When the doctor returned an hour later I had the extraction done without anæsthetics.

Soon after my experience at Maperi, news drifted through of yet another big strike at a place called Mawoga, on the main road to Lake Rukwa. In a short while I found myself at this centre, where there were already all the indications of a major rush. Mawoga did not differ much from either of the previous strikes, except perhaps that conditions here were even worse than before. When, after ten days of prospecting, I still had discovered nothing worth while, I decided to strike out for the Sira River Gorge. The river higher up in the mountainous area had previously yielded several hundred ounces of gold, and I figured out that a lot of fine gold must have washed down into the flats below. Careful examination of the river-bed below the gorge revealed a pool some 70 feet deep.

By this time I had availed myself of all the literature procurable on the subject of alluvial digging. There were several cases on record where river-pools had yielded deposits of over 1,000 oz. of gold—one such case was recorded only a few months earlier in Kenya. Pannings above the pool showed excellent results, and the indications were that I had struck a winner. A more careful survey of the general situation indicated the necessity of diverting the flow of water from the river-bed. But diverting the stream for a mile or more, installing power pumps, and erecting water-proof barriers above the pool was a formidable undertaking which would require a lot of time, work, and money. In due course I formed a syndicate of three, and a fortnight later 500 native labourers were working at top speed to complete the preliminary work before pumping operations could begin.

A month later a mile-long trench, 15 feet deep, was completed and the last barrier across the river sunk to bed-rock and 2,000 bags filled with earth packed in to prevent seepage. The pumps were being connected, and in a few days one of the biggest projects of its kind on the Lupa would be on its way. We were already counting up the value of 1,000 oz. of gold which, at the time, amounted to something like £12,000, and expenses were calculated to amount to no more than £1,500. Within the next six weeks, we firmly believed, there would be over £10,000 to share from the venture. The rainy season had come to an end fully a month before, and it would be plain sailing from now onwards. But later that afternoon black clouds started gathering in the east. By four o'clock a heavy rain set in, and that night we suffered the heaviest storm recorded in that region for twenty years. By daybreak the river was a raging torrent and carried everything before it. We were lucky to save the pumping installation, but 2,000 bags of earth were swept out into the plains below.

This was a disastrous setback, but with £10,000 in the offing one can survive such troubles in a philosophic spirit. It was fully two weeks before we were again in a position to connect the pumps. Work started early one morning, and two power-pumps worked night and day to empty the pool. Four days later we began to haul pay-dirt. Pannings right from the beginning proved disappointing, but we all felt convinced that the gold would be located deep down.

Ten days later we realized that we had struck bottom; the pool was empty and the pay-dirt ready for sluicing. When the last of the pay-dirt went through the sluices four days later we gathered around anxiously to collect the spoils, and were horrified to find that the total recovery amounted to exactly twelve penny-weights of gold—valued at 84s. It was only then that our native headman, who had worked on the project from the beginning, calmly informed us that some three years earlier he had worked for a European who had also emptied the pool and taken lots and lots of gold from it. Our total outlay amounted to more than £1,000 and the recovery was less than £5. It was at that point that I scrapped every book on alluvial in my possession. The position was desperate. Five hundred labourers were clamouring for wages, and in the kitty there was barely £5. That night 450 labourers departed from the scene, each the proud possessor of an I.O.U. for services rendered.

The partnership was wound up and we each set out to look for pastures new. Early the next morning I left the scene of this disastrous venture on my way back to my main camp. That afternoon I was glad to meet an old friend from the Congo. To him I related the misfortune I had suffered on the Sira, hoping that he might be able to suggest something to help me out of the dire predicament.

Charlie, however, had a story to relate which appeared to be even more pathetic than my own. On the claim he was then operating he employed some 150 labourers. At first results were good, but gradually his recovery decreased. During the preceding month he was reduced to buying meal on credit from native hawkers; for some time, however, his supply had been cut off, as he had failed to meet his commitments. Charlie's claims were situated on the main pathway used by native hawkers from the Ufipa country to carry their meal for sale among the diggers in the Lupa area.

It was at the time his fortunes had reached their lowest ebb that Charlie suddenly remembered that he had a half-grown lion which he kept as a pet, and which might be of some use to help in easing the situation. As a large convoy of porters carrying maize-meal from Ufipa approached his camp one morning he released the lion from its cage. When the camp dogs rushed out to meet the convoy, the lion promptly joined issue. Charlie stoutly maintained that a week later his labourers were still picking up loads of meal the porters had dropped in their hurry to escape from the lion.

The food problem was thus satisfactorily solved for some weeks, but now the labourers were crowding round his tent; they all held two or more I.O.U.'s in respect of wages due, and were demanding payment. The situation was beginning to look ugly as Charlie slowly entered his tent. When next he appeared it was with a roll of fuse in his hands. The burning fuse was promptly tossed among the threatening labourers. Natives have a wholesome respect for explosives, and in a matter of seconds there was not a single black to be seen in the neighbourhood. ' I'll be free of this lot for a while,' remarked Charlie laconically as he poured himself another sundowner.

Charlie's methods were instructive indeed, but not very helpful to me, for I kept no pet lions nor explosives. There was nothing to be gained by staying, so I continued my journey. Arrived back at camp, I found that the situation was even worse than I had expected. The Lupa River had stopped flowing, and only isolated pools of water remained. Without running water, sluicing was impossible. The ten labourers who had brought my camp gear back were dissatisfied and sulky; like myself, they could see no quick way of getting on to payable gold. Desperate situations call for desperate methods. The situation was critical, and I was racking my brains to find a way out of this impossible impasse. It was in this desperate state of mind that I took a walk along the Lupa River one morning and discovered, not only a means of saving my own situation, but also of prolonging the life of the Lupa Goldfield for several years and improving the lot of every digger who worked the river-beds.

As I have already mentioned, gold on the Lupa was recovered mainly by panning. As I walked along the river, I came to an enormous dump of tailings where natives had previously panned ore from a rich deposit. The thought came to my mind that if one could devise a method whereby gold could be made to settle on a blanket with the minimum of water, which could be carried or hand-pumped, it would provide the means of treating ten times the amount of gravel a good panner could handle, and with less risk of loss. It was the birth of an idea, and forthwith I got the natives to mount a sluice-box on poles. An ordinary grain-bag was used to serve as a blanket, and water was carried in Debbis (four-gallon petrol tins). The ore was to be washed over a screen, and any gold there was should settle on the blanket below. For two hours we washed tailings from the dump, and at the end of that time I examined the grain-bag. There was not a trace of gold to be seen. This was the signal for the natives to call it a day. I returned to camp that afternoon weary and mentally distressed. The situation was beyond redemption.

Next morning early I got the natives to accompany me back to the river to collect the equipment. Before dismantling the sluice-box I checked over once again to make sure I had not missed anything the previous day. I was amazed to find a heavy deposit of gold nuggets below the screen where the gravel had dropped on the grain-bag. A quick check-up showed that I had recovered 4 oz. of gold in two hours of work on the tailings dump. I immediately set to work to make several adjustments to the structure of the box, and that was the birth of the ' Debbi Box ' on the Lupa. It also earned for me the flattering sobriquet of ' Debbi-Box John '. For more than a month I played the lone wolf. No one knew how, or what, I was doing, but at the end of that time my recovery figure reached the respectable total of 140 oz. of gold—all recovered from tailings dumps—which gold panners had lost previously.

The Debbi Box was a simple but effective device. It needed only four natives to operate and move about the field. It proved also a quick and effective method of prospecting gravel deposits. Within a short time the Debbi Box was in operation over the entire field. One enterprising digger employed no fewer than 700 natives using 175 boxes. Each box was rated good for at least 1 dwt. of gold per day; frequently a box returned more than an ounce per day—depending on the richness of the gravel. There was the case of the Vogel brothers, who were operating an ancient river-bed a mile from the nearest water. A panner could do only eight pans per day. The Vogels had not heard about the Debbi Box when I passed their camp on my way to the Sira River. I remained with them a few days, and organized a box for them. They had long since reached the ' Buffalo ' stage, and their situation was desperate. On the third day we were watching gravel being washed by the natives when there was a sudden shout from one of the washers as he came rushing towards us. In his hand he carried what was up to that time the second largest nugget ever found on the Lupa: 84 oz. of pure gold.

The sudden change in my fortunes with the aid of the Debbi Box induced me once again to try the Sira River at a point a mile below where I had suffered the disastrous loss on the pool. There were several ancient river-beds running parallel to each other, and I decided that the fourth of these beds was the one which carried the original deposit of gold. My camp was pitched under an enormous tree which grew in what must have been the first and original course of the river many centuries earlier. I was still working on the theories contained in the books I had read previously, and felt convinced I was on the right trail.

During the next three weeks I dug a trench 40 feet deep across the river-bed, and came to barren bed-rock. There was not a trace of gold. It was again time to look for pastures new. Five miles down the river I had better luck, and remained there for a month. At the end of that time I decided to return to my main camp. Late that afternoon I came to the spot where I had made the deep trench across the river. The

F

scene that met my eyes here was staggering. Some sixty tents had already been erected, and there were all the indications of a big rush. Inquiries revealed that there had been a rich strike. An old prospector had followed my trail to the spot where I had camped, and under the very tree where I had lived for more than a month he had struck it rich. Previously I had thrown away all the books I had treating the subject of alluvial gold. It was time now for a thorough brain-washing: it was time, in fact, to consider seriously whether the game was worth the candle.

CHAPTER VIII

I CHANGE VOCATION

AFTER THE SECOND disastrous attempt on the Sira River, I once again returned to my main camp. I felt it was time to take stock and decided what to do for the future. The catering contract which was responsible for my remaining on the Lupa had fallen through. A careful balancing of accounts showed that in six months, during which time I had suffered two major setbacks, I was some £350 to the good. This result was not at all bad if judged by Lupa standards, but the life, with its uncertainties and hardships, had left a bad impression on me, and I began to think of an old friend of mine who had obtained a licence to buy gold. He was doing reasonably well, but limited capital restricted his activities.

In the past he had mentioned to me that one could earn a far better living, with greater security, in the buying business. A fair amount of capital, however, was necessary. I decided I would call on this good friend and explore the possibilities of forming a partnership. Apart from the £350, I also possessed mining equipment and other assets which would boost my capital to some £800. In addition, I also held two very promising claims which, with careful supervision, could possibly make an important difference to my financial position. These claims, I decided, would have to be shelved for some time if I could arrange the partnership.

A few days later I called on my friend. His position had not altered materially, and extra capital was still needed. When I left him that night we had come to an arrangement, and I figured as a full half-share partner in the gold-buying business in consideration of the payment of a sum of £750.

From now on I felt certain life would be easier and more secure. The licence we held permitted us to buy gold directly from any licensed digger. Our commission charges were considerably higher than those of the bank at Mbeya. The extra charges, however, were willingly paid, as our service saved diggers the long journey to Mbeya and enabled sellers to convert even the smallest amount of gold into ready cash. It also reduced the serious risks attending regular visits to Mbeya, where bottle-stores and bars often proved too strong a temptation for a man possessed of cash. On the field there were no bottle-stores or bars.

I now started on my rounds as a gold-buyer. One had to keep a finger on the pulse of the field and be on the spot wherever a lucky strike was reported. There was also the routine work of rounding up the diggers wherever they might be, or whatever their fortunes. It was a busy life, but a paying proposition, and, above all, it also helped me to realize more fully how truly hopeless the life of the average digger on the goldfield can be. I could easily fill a volume with the tales of sorrow and misery I listened to on my travels. But I would rather relate some of the humorous incidents.

Shortly after I had started in the new venture I received news of a strike on the Upper Lupa, where a number of my old Congo friends were still settled. I decided to be on the spot before the gold could find its way to Mbeya. On my arrival there I learned that it was one of my best friends of Congo days who had struck it rich. Tim had been on the field for more than a year, and this was his first strike. Luck attended his efforts when he opened up an old trench, and within an hour of beginning operations he had picked up a 45-oz. slug of gold.

Tim was an Irishman with whom I had done considerable hunting in the early days in the Back Congo. He was noted for his generosity and extreme fondness for 'Scotch'. By the time I reached his camp he had already disposed of the nugget, and the tent bore ample evidence of the celebrations which had followed his strike. Tim had only a few ounces of gold to dispose of when I called on him, but he informed me that two of his friends—Jock, a Scotsman, and Pirelli, an Italian—who were working in partnership a mile away, had also struck it lucky. They had in fact celebrated the occasion with him the previous night, and had only left during the early hours of the morning. If I made it a point to reach their camp by daybreak, I would be in good time to buy whatever gold they had on hand.

I decided to spend the night with Tim and to leave for Jock's camp before dawn next day. The occasion proved to be anything but peaceful; my rest was disturbed not only by Tim, who frequently burst into song, but also by a pride of lions who roared intermittently through the night.

Just before dawn I set out on my journey by motor-bike on the way to Jock's camp, which I reached a few minutes later. There was no response to my shouting and knocking, and in the end I managed to stir up the cook, who informed me that his master had again gone back to Tim's camp the previous evening and had not yet returned. As I had spent that night with Tim, and Jock had failed to put in an appearance, I felt certain that he had come to grief with the lions we had heard the night before.

I immediately raised the alarm, and together with some twenty natives set out on the trail to find what was left of Jock and his friend, who had again accompanied him. The cook had meanwhile informed me that there had been a lot of drinking the night before, and that both Jock and his friend were not only very much the worse for wear when they left camp, but that they had also taken an ample supply of whisky with them. The trail bore all the evidence of the extent to which the pair had indulged. For nearly a mile they had stuck to the footpath as best they could, but at that point they had taken a wrong turning which led deep into dense forest. As we followed their trail deeper into the bush I had no doubt they had fallen prey to the lions. My fears were allayed, however, when nearly a mile farther on, we found the pair fast asleep in a fond embrace, on the lower branches of a large tree.

They were duly awakened, and Jock forthwith explained that whilst they were walking on the path which they believed would take them to Tim's camp, a lion had suddenly set up a loud roar quite close to them. Unarmed, and with this imminent danger now threatening them, the couple had made a headlong rush for the nearest tree where they could find safety high up in its branches. Arriving there, they had experienced the greatest difficulty in climbing out of reach of the lion. Whilst they were struggling to scale the tree, the lion had several times given full rein to its vocal chords, but in the end they had managed to find safety well out of reach of any troublesome lion, and gone off into a peaceful sleep.   It was in this position that we found them on the branch which was not more than four feet from the ground.

The incongruity of the situation must have struck home very forcibly, for later in the day Jock assured me that it was all a joke at the expense of Pirelli.   He himself was well aware of the fact that a roaring lion is never really dangerous, but Pirelli, who was a ' green horn ', did not know this.   When later I helped to dress his hands where the skin had been badly cut during his efforts to climb the tree, I could not help remarking to him that he had carried the joke a bit too far. Pirelli's version of the night's events are not fit for publication.

I collected 30 oz. of gold in this camp and then went on to the next, where the humour was of a grimmer nature.   Bill was operating a claim where he had been doing very well for several weeks.   On my arrival there I found a police officer in attendance.   He was taking statements from four of Bill's friends.   Of Bill himself there was no sign.

After the officer had departed I listened to an account of the events that had led to the inquiry I had just witnessed.   During recent weeks Bill had done so well that he was in a position to invest in a new car.   The car was promptly loaded with an ample supply of whisky, and on his arrival back in camp Bill had invited his four closest friends to come along and celebrate the occasion.   By the end of the second night of celebrating it was considered time to call a halt, and Bill had obligingly offered to drive his friends home.   During that hectic drive he had lost control of the car somewhere on the road and driven it over an embankment.   Bill was killed outright, whilst the other members of the party sustained only slight injuries.   The car was a complete wreck.   The accident was duly reported to the nearest D.C., who, after examining the scene of the accident, had given permission for Bill to be buried.

At this stage of its development the Lupa still looked upon undertakers as an expensive and unnecessary luxury.   Coffins, when needed, were fashioned out of rough native timber which grew in the vicinity, and from planks of any size and thickness. There is no record of any occupant ever having protested against this procedure.

Bill's corpse was laid out on a table in the store; a tree from which planks could be cut was felled and the services of a native carpenter enlisted to prepare a coffin. Whilst this was being done the four friends returned to the dining-room, there to indulge in more drinking. After an all-night effort the carpenter managed to complete the job by ten o'clock next morning. The coffin was duly approved and the lid nailed down. When the D.C. arrived later in the afternoon the four friends were still busy drowning their sorrows. Native porters were hurriedly sent for and the coffin carried to the grave, where it was forthwith interred.

After the ceremony the friends decided to return to Bill's camp to give further expression to their grief. Later that night, when the whisky supply had run out, the cook was sent for to bring fresh supplies from the store. A few moments later he appeared in the doorway in a highly excited state to announce that his master was back in the store. It was only then that Bill's friends realized that they had forgotten to place his body in the coffin and that the service earlier in the day had been conducted over an empty coffin. The police officer I had seen there on my arrival had come to conduct an inquiry into this latest development in the matter of the death and burial of Bill. The inquiry completed, they would have to await further instructions in the matter. As I prepared to quit the scene, the cook was once again on his way to the store for a further supply of gloom-dispeller and Bill was still lying in state.

It was not long after I had started in the buying business that another invention, the ' dry-blower ', made its appearance on the field. This ingenious contraption, born of despair, like my Debbi Box, operated a series of fans which fitted into a carefully balanced frame and launder. The average dry-blower, operated by a gang of fifteen or twenty labourers, could easily handle twenty tons of gravel in a day. It needed no water and could be worked in the hills and other areas where previously the lack of water had made mining operations impossible. The standard of recovery was very high and compared favourably with that of the Debbi Box, which by now had been subjected to numerous improvements. The field was wearing a new coat from the financial point of view, and the average turnover must have been at least five times as high as before.

Several diggers now sported the latest models in cars and trucks and the standard of living was correspondingly higher. This new trend had induced several competitors to enter the buying field. Gold was more plentiful, but competition was much keener.

Our organization was doing very well, so much so that my partner decided to take three months' leave in the south. It was only a fortnight after his departure that I experienced another major setback which finally led to the complete disruption of the organization we had so carefully built. Shortly before I left the Congo I had suffered a severe injury to my leg. The injury had to all intents and purposes healed completely before my departure, but now there was a sudden recurrence of the trouble in a very much aggravated form. In a few days I was confined to bed in a small camp miles away from any help. The trouble soon became so acute that I had to send for a doctor from Mbeya, 65 miles away. The doctor duly arrived and put me through a thorough examination. His diagnosis made it clear that my condition was much worse than I had expected. I was suffering from a bad attack of phlebitis. All the doctor could do for me was to recommend large doses of aspirin when the pain became unbearable, and present his account. I had to remain in bed until the swelling had disappeared.

The only assistance I could depend on was from an old native named Dan, who in the distant past had once worked for a European as cook. Actually, Dan claimed that he was present on the occasion of the meeting between Livingstone and Stanley, which took place somewhere about 1875. At that time, he contended, he was a youth of fifteen or seventeen years of age. There was nothing in the appearance of Dan to belie his statement; in fact he stoutly maintained that he had first learned cooking in Dr. Livingstone's kitchen. As time went on I became convinced that Dan's story was true in every respect but one—he was no youth, but a man well on in years at the date of this historical meeting. Dan's memory was appalling: he forgot everything I told him immediately I had finished talking, and remembered only when it was payday, or when money for rations became due. His cooking was on a par with his memory, and I have no doubt that his contribution in Dr. Livingstone's kitchen must have hastened the great man's end.

I often needed Dan's help at night, but once he had fallen into a sleep nothing short of a charge of dynamite could awaken him. As I was unable to move out of my bed, I had to scheme out a method whereby I could awaken him when I needed him. I had managed to procure a reel of builder's twine. Dan slept only a few feet from my bed, and before he turned in for the night one end of the twine was tied to one of his toes, and the other end to a four-gallon tin of water which was mounted on a bracket above his head. If pulling string number one brought no results, I would resort to number two. In this manner I managed on occasions to stir him out of bed.

At daybreak one morning, after a sleepless night, I felt inclined for toast and coffee. After I had resorted to string No. 2, Dan began to show signs of life, and before long a fire was burning briskly at the foot of my bed, but a little while later the place was in dead silence and there was no sign of a fire. With some difficulty I managed to raise myself to a sitting position to see what was happening. Dan had once again dropped off into a deep sleep, his feet were stretched out towards the fire, and between the toes of each foot he had firmly wedged a piece of toast—now burnt as black as coal. My breakfast was on its way.

There was only one butcher on the field, 25 miles from my camp, and what he sold as meat could have passed as high-quality boot leather in any other part of the world. It was only by mincing the product that it could be rendered edible. Minced stew is a dish that soon palls on one, and it was to escape from the daily stew that I one day suggested to Dan that he should change the diet and try to prepare rissoles for me. Dan knew all about rissoles—in fact Dr. Livingstone, who must have lived under conditions similar to my own, was very fond of them, and had taught him how to prepare them. But Dan's method of rendering the meat into round balls was novel, to say the least. For this purpose he divested himself of his shirt; handsful of meat were then taken from a dish and rolled into balls on his naked stomach. As water was so scarce in this area that there was hardly ever enough for domestic needs for myself, I knew that Dan did not often indulge in the luxury of a bath—and even if he did . . .?

But for all that Dan was a loyal and willing servant, and very sympathetic towards me. I put up with his many short-comings as long as I could, but the final break came one morning when I had got myself into a sitting position again and watched him prepare my morning coffee, and found him straining the brew through one of his socks. The coffee had been suspect for some days, and I did not have to look further to find the explanation. In adverse circumstances one is often compelled to put up with a lot, but Dan's cooking was definitely beyond all endurance. He was relieved of his post as cook and the position filled by a friend of his whom he recommended very strongly. The resulting memories are too painful to relate, but I managed to survive another four months. By this time the swelling had gone down and I was able to walk short distances without too much pain.

My partner had still not returned from his holiday, and whatever connexion we had built up in the gold-buying business was irretrievably lost. The financial position had once again become precarious, and I decided I would work the two claims I had previously shelved, with the new method of dry-blowing. A week later I was carried to the spot, and within a few days work was in full swing. For once the evil fortune which had dogged my steps for so long seemed to relent. Results were good from the outset, and at the end of three weeks I found myself in pocket to the tune of £1,250 after all expenses had been paid. But there were indications that the claims were petering out, and I decided to accept a cash offer of £500 for the lot. My leg was rapidly healing and my health was much improved. The nights of pain when rats made merry in my bed and ran over my face, the days of toe-baked toast and stomach-rolled rissoles were relegated to the chapter of unpleasant memories. There was no point in tempting fortune any further. Even under the best and most favourable conditions alluvial digging is always a game of chance, and luck plays a predominant part. I had had my share of both good and bad luck, and I decided to call it a day. It was again time to take stock and decide what to do for the future.

By this time the goldfield had expanded enormously, and

now sported a post office, hospital, hotel, and numerous Indian stores. News of the field had spread far and wide. Mining companies were sending consultants to report on various properties and in two cases companies had already started reef-mining. News came to me that one of these companies required a secretary-accountant, and I immediately applied for the position. My knowledge of accounting, strictly speaking, did not justify my soliciting the post, but I did not think it necessary to emphasize the point. There were, in any case, no out-of-work accountants on the Lupa at the time, and when I was called to the manager's office a few days later my application was accepted after I have given a definite assurance that I would be able to manage the job.

I was due to start work at the beginning of the following month, which left me just two weeks to brush up on accounts and obtain all the instruction I could. I immediately consulted my old friend Tim, of Upper Lupa fame; he had once held the position of chief accountant in Barclay's Bank in South Africa. Tim was quite willing to give me all the assistance I needed on condition that he did not ' work dry ' whilst the lessons were in progress. When I took up my appointment, which fortunately was delayed for another fortnight, I had quite a reasonable knowledge of the routine side of the work. I then took a correspondence course with a well-known college in the South, and rapidly settled down to my new profession of secretary-accountant, which also included such minor functions as acting manager when the manager was away—which happened quite frequently—chief storekeeper, compound manager, public relations officer when miners and management were at loggerheads, father confessor to the blacks in their matrimonial and domestic disputes—in fact, a glorified mining general factotum. My duties also included visits to different parts of the field where the Company held development options, and records had also to be kept. The working days often amounted to eighteen or more hours, but this did not worry me unduly; I liked the work and somehow managed to crowd in the hours necessary for study.

The main property was rapidly expanding, and we soon reached the stage where it was compulsory for us to employ a full-time medical officer. It was left for me to explore the possibilities of finding a medical man suitable and willing to accept the post. Here again my efforts were directed into a channel which brought me the acquaintance and friendship of one of the most amazing characters I have ever met—the subject of the ensuing chapter.

CHAPTER IX

MICE, MEN, AND CANCER

As the subject-matter of this chapter, which deals with the treatment and cure of cancer, is contentious and likely to provoke dissent from those who are more conversant with the subject than I am, I would make my position clear at the outset. I am no authority on the subject, and know nothing whatever about the medical aspects of the healing of cancer other than the facts I record here. In the case of Father Ortz, whose case I have fully related, I saw the official documents from medical institutions in East Africa, the Belgian Congo, and South Africa. In each case Father Ortz was certified as suffering from malignant cancer. In the case of the report from South Africa it was stated definitely that Father Ortz was suffering from cancer in an advanced state and that he was incurable. The report further added that he was permitted to return to Tanganyika at his own request, as he wished to spend his remaining days in the country to which he had devoted his life's work, and there was considerable apprehension as to whether Father Ortz could survive a journey back there.

These reports were sent to the Father Superior of the White Fathers Mission at Uruwira station, with which Mission Father Ortz had for years been associated. I myself was in daily contact with the Fathers of the Mission at that period and had access to these reports as they came in. Four months later I again saw the reports from the three institutions I have previously mentioned. In each case they stated emphatically that Father Ortz was completely free of all traces of cancer.

If the facts I am about to relate are inconsistent with medical belief, it would be interesting to speculate as to why such contradictory reports emanated from all three institutions in a matter of only four months. It would be strange indeed for all three, acting independently, to affirm that the patient was suffering from cancer in the first place, and that he was com-

pletely free of the disease in the second, if such were not
actually the case. I am concerned only in recording the facts
as they came to my notice. Having thus cleared the decks, I
continue with my story from where I left off at the end of the
preceding chapter.

Finding a doctor who would be prepared to take medical
charge of a mining camp all but cut off from civilization, in a
country where doctors were in short supply even in the popu-
lous centres, savoured very much of finding the proverbial
needle in a haystack. It would need a miracle, and I had all
but given up in despair when, sitting in the lounge in the
Mbeya Hotel one evening, I was introduced to two German
doctors who had just arrived in the country. They were both
graduates from the University of Jena, and, being of Jewish
origin, they had fled from the Nazi persecutions in Germany.
The political set-up in Tanganyika, under the League of
Nations, offered them sanctuary, and they had come out to
that country to examine the prospects of settling down in their
profession.

The miracle had happened!

When we parted company that night, the elder of the two
doctors had accepted my proposition, and we had reached a
tentative agreement whereby the matter of opening a joint
medical centre on our property would be considered at a later
date. The provisional agreement I had entered into with
Dr. X provided for him to start as medical officer for the mine
within ten days, by which time a long-term engagement would
be ready for signature. Dr. X duly presented himself on the
property on the appointed date. In the meanwhile I had
persuaded the management to accept the proposition of the
medical centre, and by so doing I had enlisted not one, but
two highly specialized doctors from one of the most famous
universities in Europe. Their medical equipment, including
X-Ray installation, was hastily brought up from Dar-es-
Salaam, and in due course the project was on its way. It was
a far cry from the days when I took my injection through a
pair of khaki trousers and dug the remnants of a tooth from my
jaw-bone.

The association between Dr. X and myself was a happy one,
and ere long we were on terms of close friendship. It was in

the capacity of friend, more than medical officer, that he called on me one day and asked me to assist him in his efforts to carry on research work which was interrupted in Europe at a time when success was assured. He did not tell me to which field his researches were directed. For the moment he was anxious that I should help him to procure several dozens of white mice. I was only too happy to help him in any way I could, but it was necessary to explain to him that scores of white mice were not so easily obtainable in that part of Tanganyika. They would have to be imported from South Africa, brought up by air, and taken delivery of immediately on arrival at Mbeya. He fully appreciated all the difficulties, but seemed quite content that, in addition to the multitude of duties which claimed my attention, he had loaded one more on to me.

The difficulties and problems I encountered in securing a supply of white mice would be of no interest to the reader; suffice it to say that it was fully two months before we collected the first consignment at Mbeya. A further, and final, consignment arrived ten days later, and after I had arranged for these to be collected, I felt free for a while to attend to other matters which required my personal supervision. Occasionally I would see the doctor and inquire after the health of the mice, always to be assured that they were doing very well.

One day, towards the middle of the month, when the pressure of work had eased, I again met the doctor, and after once more being assured that the mice were doing very well, I mentioned that I would be interested to know more about the research work on which he was engaged. Apparently this was a development the doctor had keenly anticipated, for he forthwith assured me of his eagerness for me to take a more active interest in his work. I would be welcome to call on him at any time convenient to me and watch the progress he was making. Just previous to this the doctor had asked me to obtain a week-old calf for him, which he wanted to be delivered alive at his house. The request was promptly attended to, and did not puzzle me in any way, as I concluded that his taste had run to veal.

A day or two after receiving the last invitation I decided I would call on the doctor and see what he was doing. He was happy to see me, and immediately took me to a number of cages in which different lots of mice were kept. At the door of each cage was a card on which daily observations were entered. Approaching a cage at the end of the line, he explained that ' here we have mice now almost completely recovered from a dose of cancer I have given them '. Following the line of cages, I was given a description of the progress the various inmates were making against ' the cancer I have given them '. For a moment I believed the man had taken leave of his senses and began to wonder where I would find a brain specialist to attend to him.

The fact remained, however, that in each case he would remove a patient and show me a cancerous growth at that particular stage of its development. The realization of what I was seeing had a staggering impact on my mind. The idea of seeing these poor creatures with their cancerous growths, the exquisite care with which he pointed out the cancers in their various stages of development, completely nauseated me. Either I was in the presence of a demon who derived pleasure from observing these helpless creatures suffer the tortures of hell, or I was witnessing a genius at work. After we had completed the round and each stage had been carefully explained to me, the doctor suggested that I join him in his lounge for a drink. ' A strong neat brandy, please, doctor,' I replied when asked what I preferred. I needed that brandy to settle my stomach and steady my nerves.

Once seated in comfort, the conversation immediately reverted to the subject of cancer. The doctor produced numerous newspapers with headlines in big, black, heavy type. Each referred to the new theory of the cause and cure for cancer. Readers in South Africa, where I am writing this, will remember the prominence given to the subject in the local press a few years before the outbreak of the Second World War. This publicity suddenly ceased, and no more was heard about the German claims that they had found a cure for cancer. The reason, as I have previously explained, was that, like so many other Jews in Germany, Dr. X became a fugitive from Nazi persecution, and with his disappearance from Germany the publicity, as also the research work he was doing, disappeared from that part of the world.

In addition to the newspapers, Dr. X produced many letters from medical institutions in Germany referring to the work in which he was engaged. A case mentioned in his documents completely staggered me. It referred to the treatment and care of his (Dr. X's) own mother. He explained that he had treated her for cancer and removed part of the stomach ten years earlier. She was still alive and doing as well as could be expected at the time of his departure from Germany. To create a cancer and then to cure that same cancer was something very unusual, whatever may be said to the contrary. I felt that the man at least knew what he was doing. The prominent publicity given to the subject in the German Press, the numerous documents he had shown me—all these could not be chimeras of a diseased mind. And how could one explain the practical demonstration he had given me with the mice only a few minutes earlier? The theory, which I had not heard up to then, was as thought-provoking as anything I had seen up to that moment. I give it for what it is worth:

'In India,' said the doctor, 'with its teeming millions, in China, in Japan, in Russia, in Asia, and here in Africa, we have vast populations, running into hundreds of millions. The incidence of cancer in these countries is so small that it is completely negligible. Here in Africa the position is even more striking. Cancer among the European population all over Africa is definitely on the increase; and in many cases alarmingly so. By contrast, the native population, which now increases at a more rapid rate than ever before in the history of Africa, is to all intents and purposes entirely free of cancer. Such statistics as I have available go to show that among the natives cancer is almost completely unknown. As you go higher in the scale, there is a proportionate increase in the incidence of the disease. How, then, must we explain this startling, but demonstrable fact?

'It is the food, my friend; it is the food. The scientist and the botanist are creating cancer all over the world today wherever they interfere with the natural structure of plants and seeds. The Burbanks have given us ten grains of corn where only one grew before. In so doing they have altered the natural structure of the corn-seed. They will feed thousands more on the same acreage, but they will also kill hundreds more with cancer. When the natural structure of the plants

G

and cereals we eat is altered, it has a detrimental effect on the glands in the human system, and that in turn produces cancer. I give cancer by glandular treatment and I take it away by glandular treatment. At this stage of my experiment each individual case is treated on its merits. I watch reactions and I increase or decrease the strength of the doses as required. Some day I hope to have a standard cure for all cancers. That day may never be, but it is certain that I can, and have, cured many cases to which I have given my personal attention. In the back room there are several mice, healthy and well; if you will come with me and select as many as you wish, I will guarantee to produce cancer in each of them within forty-eight hours.'

I did not go to the back room. I did not wish to select healthy animals in order that they might be inflicted with cancer. Earlier I had seen at least twenty animals suffering in different stages of cancer. The proof was there; I needed no other.

The evening, so far as I was concerned, was drawing to a close. If the opportunity presented itself again I would spend hours more listening to the doctor expounding his theories, but for one night I had seen and heard enough. I would go home and think it all over. Yes, what he had said so far as Africa is concerned was undoubtedly true. I had never thought of it before, but now that it had been brought to my notice I had to admit that in all the years I had wandered about in the African bush—Rhodesia, Belgian Congo, French Congo, Ubangi, Sudan, Uganda, Kenya, Tanganyika, Nyasaland—and had walked through all these countries, mixing freely with the native inhabitants, I had never heard of a case of cancer. But Europeans in these countries were as prone to cancer as they are everywhere else. What happened in India, China, Japan, and Russia in Asia I did not know, as I had no statistics to refer to, but I had no reason to disbelieve what the doctor had told me. He certainly had pages of statistics available up to that time. Whether these figures have changed materially since then I cannot say.

From this time onwards I visited the doctor as often as my duties and opportunities permitted. His research in cancer quickly became known in the district, and patients were soon being treated on the spot. During the time he was associated with our Company he treated ten cases, most of which came from Kenya and other parts of Tanganyika, and one from England. Nine of these were cured, and the tenth—an advanced case of stomach cancer—died.

After that I visited the doctor regularly, and on each occasion he discussed with me the problems associated with a universal cure for cancer. A great deal of what he told me was too technical for me to understand. But what I could gather from him was that one of the major problems had to do with hormones in the human system. If more was known about this subject it would be much easier to find a universal cure for malignant cancer. Time went on, and the doctor worked continuously on his experiments. Then, when war broke out, everything came to a sudden stop. The doctor was, in fact, a stateless alien, but the fact that he was a German national up to the time of his escape from Nazi Germany complicated matters. He was forced to resign his position and report to the authorities in Dar-es-Salaam. There, to all intents and purposes, he was treated as an enemy subject and had to undergo regular surveillance. He had to submit to many restrictions and his research work was once again interrupted.

In the earlier part of the war gold was a number one priority and our mine continued operations without hindrance. Later, however, when Lease Lend came into force, the position suddenly changed. In Tanganyika gold dropped to number seven priority. It was not long before the supplies position made it impossible for us to continue. The property went into liquidation and I was appointed liquidator. The liquidation was completed in 1943, and shortly after that I took up a position with another mining concern producing lead.

From the day of his departure from the Lupa area I heard no more from, or about, my doctor friend. Now, on arrival at the new property, I was surprised and happy to find that he had been posted to this mine by the Tanganyika Government as medical officer. In my new post I was in charge of all stores and supplies, and in this capacity I had frequent dealings with the doctor. Our friendship continued on similar lines to those that prevailed earlier. The other members of the community, however, ostracized him and subjected him to many indignities on account of his German origin. He told me that the years since the outbreak of war were among the unhappiest of his life, as he had been pushed from pillar to post and ostracized wherever he went.

In our previous discussions on cancer the doctor had told me that his cure was based mainly on the extract from glands which he removed from a very young and healthy calf. The calf was killed and every gland from its body removed and passed through a mincer. The mass was then left in pure alcohol for an hour, after which it was passed through filters and the residue discarded. The rest of the experiment is not known to me.

Whilst sitting on the veranda of my house one afternoon, a team of native porters stopped outside my door. They were carrying a young calf in a large packing-case. The case had been carefully closed with mosquito gauze to protect the animal from tsetse-flies, the area through which it was carried being one of the worst infected areas in all Africa. The natives had stopped at my house to inquire where the doctor was to be found; in fact they carried a letter addressed to him. I was puzzled, for I realized that the animal had something to do with the doctor's activities in cancer research, but as there were no mice on the property, I was left wondering what it was all about. Later that evening I called on the doctor, and in reply to my inquiry he informed me that a serious cancer case was due to arrive that night, and that treatment would commence immediately. The patient in question was Father Ortz, who had returned from South Africa in the circumstances I have related earlier. The calf would be killed early the next morning, and I was welcome to come and see him extract the glands. The meat would go to the mine mess, and the mine chef had been instructed to call for it.

Early the following morning we watched the doctor dissect the carcass and treat the various glands. We remained for an hour or more discussing the case, and at the end of that time the residue of the glands was removed from alcohol and thrown into an empty box outside an open window. A few minutes later the doctor rushed out and chased off some fowls which were eating the discarded residue. He seemed very perturbed on his return, and went on to explain that all the birds that had eaten from the residue were certain to contract cancer. Within two days, he asserted, their crops would be eaten away with cancer. None of us took this statement very seriously, and before we left his house the incident was forgotten.

On the afternoon of the second day the doctor called on me at my office and suggested I accompany him to his house again. In the backyard were the hens, all sitting cooped up in a corner of an outhouse. ' They have all got cancer,' the doctor remarked as he threw a handful of maize to them. As we stood watching the hens feeding, the doctor asked me to watch their crops. There was no doubt, as fast as they picked up the maize, the grains poured out of their crops. In each case there was a vivid red sore apparent, and I was assured that they would all die in a day or two. To save them un-necessary suffering, the birds were destroyed.

The treatment of Father Ortz was due to commence that same evening, and I was invited to accompany the doctor to the Father's quarters. Father Ortz himself was a Mission doctor, and I had been introduced to him the day after his arrival. He was obviously in a dying state, and told me so. His head was heavily bandaged and he informed me that the cancer had eaten away the entire ear and had worked its way deep into the orifice. Soon it would reach the brain, and that would be the end. He was quite resigned to his fate. The trouble, he informed me, had started with a pimple on the ear, and, being a medical practitioner, he had suspected cancer. His suspicions were confirmed in Dar-es-Salaam, where he spent some time in hospital. He was then sent to Elisabethville in the Belgian Congo, where he received radium treatment for a while. He did not respond to treatment, and was then sent to Pretoria, South Africa. In spite of the expert treatment he received there, his condition continued to deteriorate, and he was informed that nothing could be done to stop the advance of the cancer, which would soon reach the brain. A report to this effect was also sent to the Father Superior at Uruwira Mission in Tanganyika. At the request of Father Ortz, the Mission had taken the necessary steps for him to be brought back to Tanganyika. The Mission was only about 20 miles from the property where Dr. X was employed, and the doctor frequently attended cases there. It was during a visit to the Mission that the case of Father Ortz was first mentioned to him and resulted in the Father being sent to the mine for treatment.

That night I accompanied the doctor, and was present when the bandages were removed. As Father Ortz had told me, nothing remained of the left ear, and in the head there was a horrible cavity. The sight completely nauseated me, and it was difficult to understand how the patient had survived such a terrible affliction. I left immediately the doctor had made his first examination.

After this I visited the Father daily. At first there were no visible signs of improvement, but gradually he started to rally. The bandages were removed every three days, but I was not present on these occasions until the tenth day. There was then a notable sign of improvement in the ear. Dr. X was quite confident that he could cure the cancer, but he held small hope for the patient, whose main trouble he now considered was not the cancer, but radium poisoning, brought on by over-doses administered during the treatment in Elisabethville. There were already signs of dropsy, and severe swelling of the legs had set in.

It was quite two months later that I was again present when the bandages were removed. Apart from the missing member, there was not a trace of cancer. The entire area where before there was an open cavity now had hair growing over it. Father Ortz stated definitely that he suffered no pain or any other inconvenience in so far as the ear was concerned, but he was by now suffering from acute dropsy. That night the doctor took samples of the entire area that had been affected with cancer previously, and the samples were sent to the three institutions where Father Ortz had been treated previously. The verdict in each case was that there was no sign of cancer. By this time the Father was being subjected to daily tappings to relieve the swelling caused by dropsy. Three weeks later he died from the result of a heart attack.

It was not long after this that Dr. X was once again instructed to report at Tabora, from where he was eventually transferred back to Dar-es-Salaam. It was whilst he was at this latter place that the war finally came to an end. Shortly after this

I left the property for an extensive tour in the Rift Valley on Locust Control, and it is now more than four years ago since I last heard from the doctor in Dar-es-Salaam, where he was then practising. The facts I have recorded here are true in every respect and can be vouched for by several responsible persons. I make no attempt to explain anything. That Dr. X could induce and cure cancer of a particular type is undoubtedly true. It is certain also that, after he had induced cancer and left it without treatment, the results were always fatal. This was proved in the case of the mice with which he experimented earlier. That Father Ortz was suffering from a cancer which would have led to fatal results but was definitely cured is also true.

At the time I started writing this chapter I was on the point of leaving for Europe. On the boat via the East Coast I completed the typing, and hoped to present the script to Dr. X in Dar-es-Salaam, where I believed he was still living. On my arrival at his old address I was informed that he had left for Europe some four years ago and was last heard of in Russia. That did not surprise me, for I knew that he resented the many indignities he had suffered in East Africa, especially during the war period. A week later our boat docked at Port Said, where I procured the latest English newspapers. In heavy black type on the front page of one of them was an announcement that Russia had found a cure for cancer. The treatment was injections which dissolved the cancerous growth but did not harm healthy tissues. Is this merely a coincidence?

CHAPTER X

TRAINING THE CHEETAH

At the beginning of the last war, I was operating a small gold-mine in the Southern Highlands of Tanganyika. The property was over 200 miles from the nearest railway station, and with petrol and tyres almost unobtainable, the supply position soon became extremely difficult. We were forced, for the greater part, to live off the land, and it was in order to improve the food situation for the labourers that I once more set out on a hunting trip in the Sira Valley, where game was plentiful and conditions ideal for smoking and curing meat in large quantities.

I had come out prepared to spend a fortnight or longer on this safari, but I was lucky enough to catch up with a big herd of buffaloes on the second day in the field, and by the time the shooting was over I had collected four big bulls. This was all I needed, and it was late in the afternoon before all the meat was brought into camp. The next day would be devoted to cutting up the meat and making a start on smoking. That night the joints were hung over ropes which were tied to trees close to the camp. It was shortly after eight o'clock that the din started. Hyenas were howling lustily all round the camp, and then suddenly there was the grunting of a lion. Nearer and nearer the grunting came, and this was followed by a loud snarl. The next instant a complete line of meat had been pulled down into the sand. A few seconds later I lined up a big male lion in the rays of my shooting lamp and put paid to the raider's account. For the next hour or two the peace of the night was disturbed only by the hyenas, and just before midnight the watchman reported that a leopard was busy raiding the meat which had been piled in a heap after it had been pulled down by the lion. I immediately trained my lamp on to the spot and picked up a pair of eyes in its rays. At the moment of shooting I felt convinced that it was a leopard, but on examining the carcass I found that it was a male cheetah.

The shooting of this cheetah led me to one of my most interesting experiences in the bush and induced me to delay my return home for nearly a fortnight. Cheetahs have always interested me, and I had often watched them hunting down their prey on the open plains. Their speed is proverbial, but in addition they are past masters in the art of stalking. They generally hunt in pairs, and have exceptionally keen eyesight. When the prey is spotted, often from a distance of more than 500 yards, the cheetah immediately gets down flat on its stomach—the smallest objects, a patch of grass, a rock, or the stump of a tree is effectively used for cover—and when a distance of little more than 100 yards separates it from its intended victim there is a sudden rush; by the time the animal is aware of what is happening, the cheetah is within a few yards from it. There is no animal in Africa that can hold its own against a cheetah for speed. As often as not, the unequal race is terminated in a matter of seconds. The cheetah generally attacks the throat, and invariably the jugular vein is severed. Its grip is as tenacious as that of a bulldog, and the victim is accounted for in very quick time. As a feeder, the cheetah is not only dirtier—if that is possible—than the lion; it is also far more destructive. It is extremely rare for these animals to return to a kill once they have taken their fill.

Two days after the shooting of the cheetah the meat was ready for packing, and we left camp shortly after ten o'clock on our way back home. By five o'clock that afternoon we pitched camp for the night close to Galula Mission. Shortly after we had settled down, a native runner came in to report the presence of a pair of cheetahs in the vicinity and begged me to go out and shoot them—a request I promptly turned down. In subsequent conversation I gathered from the natives that there were lots of cheetahs in this particular area and, as in the case of lions, the natives here had great faith in the efficacy of cheetah fat in treating all sorts of ailments. Rubbed into the tail of domestic animals, it would guarantee immunity against tsetse bite. Mixed with lion fat and powdered vulture eyes and taken in small quantities in food it would ensure the eater all the coveted qualities of these animals—speed, strength, and keenness of eyesight.

Sitting round the camp-fire later in the evening, I received a visit from an Indian who operated a trading-store near the Mission. He was anxious to buy the skins of all the animals I had shot—the cheetah skin especially attracted his attention. After the deal was concluded we sat talking near the fire, and I gathered from my visitor that he had come out to Kenya some years earlier with a wealthy Indian to buy cheetahs to take back to India, where they were to be trained for hunting purposes. Abdullah, my visitor, informed me that he had had many years of experience in training cheetahs—a fact that interested me greatly, for, although I had often kept cheetahs as pets and several of my friends had similarly succeeded in taming them after they had been caught as cubs, none of us had ever succeeded in training them as hunters. Abdullah at first was not at all anxious to give me any information on the subject, but after a great deal of discussion he finally agreed to let me in on the secret, and went on to explain that he would need an eighteen-months-old cheetah for the purpose. If I could find a way of capturing an animal of that age he would attend to the rest. I had already been told that cheetahs were plentiful in the district, and I knew that their feeding habits do not differ much from those of the hyena, for when they are hungry they will eat meat in all stages of putrefaction. I felt that there was a reasonable chance of capturing a suitable specimen.

Early next morning my hunting natives and several local recruits were put on the job of constructing half a dozen drop door-traps. These traps take the shape of a large cage and are constructed of heavy poles. A doorway, large enough to allow an animal to enter easily, is created by hauling up a heavy log by means of a strand of wire, which, in turn, is attached to a log inside the cage to which a large piece of meat is securely tied. The trap is sprung as soon as the meat is touched. The log falls into position, and the door is effectively shut. By sunset that afternoon six traps were securely installed and baited with game-meat. On examining the traps early the next day, we found that the yield for the night was two hyenas; these were released and left to go their way. Around the other traps there were numerous tracks. In each case the animals had approached quite close to the open doors, but had been too suspicious to enter the traps. For the next few days I hunted during the day and smoked the meat, keeping the traps supplied with fresh meat.

Each night brought the usual quota of hyenas and numerous tracks around the unsprung traps. Apart from size, the tracks of a hyena and cheetah are difficult to distinguish, as in both cases the claws are semi-retractile. Several of the tracks, however, led me to believe that the cheetahs had been around to investigate, and that sooner or later they would enter the cages if they did not see the hyenas trapped. On the sixth day all the traps were blank: the hyenas were getting wise to the danger of entering. On the seventh morning the first five traps were again blank, but at the sixth trap the situation was different; for here at last we had succeeded in capturing a fine specimen of cheetah.

Abdullah had asked for a young cheetah, but the specimen now sitting growling at us inside the cage was a full-grown male. I immediately sent for Abdullah, and he appeared on the scene several hours later. I eagerly awaited his verdict, and was happy when he decided that the animal would suit his purpose. He said it would be necessary for him to feed the animal himself for several days, and after it had overcome its fear and nervousness he would enter the cage and secure it. I could not afford the time to remain longer, and it was agreed that Abdullah would keep me informed regularly how he was progressing. That afternoon the rest of the traps were broken down, and early next morning I returned home. It was ten days later before I heard from Abdullah. He had managed to remove the cheetah from the cage and it was responding well to treatment at home. He thought it would take all of six months to tame it properly and prepare it for its first hunt.

After that I heard from Abdullah regularly; he was making good progress and would let me know as soon as possible when to come out. It was seven months after we had captured the cheetah that Abdullah invited me to come out for the first trial hunt. That week-end I travelled the 70 miles to Abdullah's store, and was surprised to see the change in the cheetah. It was still tied to a chain leash, but it had completely settled down to conditions and appeared to be quite domesticated, and allowed Abdullah to pet and stroke it. The first hunt was scheduled for two days later; in the intervening time the cheetah would be deprived of all food.

When I called at Abdullah's store shortly after daybreak on the second day he was ready and waiting for me. The cheetah was still on the leash, and just before lifting it on to the back of an open vanette, Abdullah fastened a black cloth over its head, leaving only the nose uncovered. A few minutes later we were on our way. I was all set to see a trained cheetah in action for the first time. At that early hour game is plentiful on the open plains, and it was not long before we spotted a reedbuck ram feeding in the distance. The vanette was driven so as to keep us on the receiving end of the wind.

When about 300 yards separated us from the buck we came to a stop. The cheetah had already picked up the scent of the buck and was showing signs of restlessness, and began straining at the leash. The collar was slowly removed, after which the head was uncovered. In a flash the cheetah jumped from the truck and ran for a short distance and then went down flat on its stomach. From that point onwards the stalk was carried out patiently and deliberately, until only about 100 yards separated the two. The buck was still completely unaware of the danger threatening it and was grazing away from the cheetah, who had once again come to a stop. Now there was a twitching of the tail as the cheetah rose to a crouching position. In the next instant it dashed forward at full speed, and before the buck became aware of the threatening danger, only about twenty paces separated the two.

The race was on, but it was only a matter of seconds before the cheetah was at the throat of its victim and pulled it down. We rapidly drove up to the spot; the cheetah was hanging on grimly to the throat, and by the time we had descended from the truck it was all over: the buck had ceased struggling, but the cheetah still held on tenaciously. Abdullah had brought a small basin with him, and this was quickly filled with the blood which flowed from the buck's throat. The basin was then pushed under the cheetah's nose and held there firmly. A few seconds later the cheetah released its grip and started lapping up the blood. The hood was quickly replaced and the collar securely fastened. After that large pieces of meat were cut from the carcass and fed to the cheetah. The rest of the carcass was loaded on the truck and the cheetah was placed well away from it. All the way back to camp it kept up a persistent growling as it strained at its leash to get at the meat which was well beyond its reach. Back in camp the cheetah was returned to its cage, where Abdullah fed it generous portions of meat.

I had seen my first cheetah hunt, but I still did not know the secret of training the animal. On asking Abdul about it he replied, 'No man has ever trained the cheetah to hunt: it learnt that from its mother whilst still very young. It is for that reason that hunting cheetahs are caught when they are nearly or quite full grown. The secret is to tame it and to lure it away from its victim before it starts to devour it. It would be dangerous to try to drag it away from its prey by force. As soon as it starts lapping blood from the basin it should be blindfolded and allowed to continue lapping up blood until the carcass is removed.'

After that first hunt I witnessed two more successful outings in which the same procedure I have described was followed. A few months later I was forced to leave the district owing to the difficult supply position. I frequently heard from Abdullah, and he mentioned that he had taken the cheetah out on many successful hunts. The last time I heard from him he informed me that he had been offered a very good price for the cheetah and that he was seriously thinking of accepting the offer. Whether he eventually disposed of it I do not know. It was perhaps a feeling that I may claim a share in the proceeds that prompted Abdullah to ignore my subsequent letters to him.

CHAPTER XI

SCAVENGERS AND OTHERS

Of all the animals in the forest, there is none that fascinates me more than the hyena. The lion is majestic, awe-inspiring, and when he gives vent to deep-throated roaring on the open plains in the still of night, the imagination is stirred. There is no subject that will keep the uninitiated listener around the camp-fire more enthralled than stories about the lion. That is perhaps as it should be. But there have been many hundreds of nights when I have sat around the camp-fire when there were no grunts, no growls or roars to indicate the presence of the King of Beasts. On these occasions I never felt that there was something lacking or that the setting was out of place. The absence of the cry of the hyena under similar conditions, however, always made me feel that the setting was wrong, and that something essentially belonging to the bush was missing. It is for this reason that I have only on the rarest occasions, and under compulsion, killed one of these animals.

To look at, the hyena is an unprepossessing animal. To watch him at the left-over kill of a lion, leopard, or cheetah is a nauseating sight, for there is not a scrap of flesh on the carcass of any animal, even in the last stages of decay, that will come amiss to the hyena. But this is also as it should be, for the hyena fills a definite and necessary function, and that is to keep the forest free from decaying carcasses.

In a chapter on Lions in *African Buffalo Trails* I wrote that the hyena, unlike the lion, is not a cannibal. This statement was immediately challenged by several readers who held different views. They asserted that there were many recorded cases of hyenas practising not only cannibalism, but that they have also been known to turn man-eaters. Whereas it is never good policy to be too dogmatic about the habits of animals, especially carnivoræ, I still maintain that during my forty years in the bush in Central Africa I never came across one case of cannibalism among hyenas. That they may turn man-eater under extreme hunger is quite possible.   I was once called out in the middle of the night to shoot a starving native dog which had resorted to man-eating as a result of hunger. That dog would have eaten anything, from a human being downwards, but that is no reason for anyone to assume that domestic dogs are man-eaters or cannibals in normal circumstances.

During, and shortly after, the native Matabele Rebellion in Southern Rhodesia there were several cases of man-eating hyenas reported, but here also the circumstances were not normal.   The habit was undoubtedly acquired as a result of the fact that during that period corpses of natives killed in action were not always promptly or properly buried.   That a hyena will devour a putrefying human body if left in the open I have no doubt.   But that he will deliberately attack a human being to appease his hunger I do not believe.   There was, however, one famous case in Tanganyika some years ago when a murderer nearly escaped the consequences of his crime by attributing the death of a native to man-eating hyenas.   In this case only the skull of the missing man was found and there were definite indications that the rest of the body had been eaten by hyenas.   It was as the result of painstaking inquiries by a native detective that the murderer was eventually exposed. Had he taken the precaution to reduce the skull, there would have been no traces left and the victim would have been written off as lost, as so often happens in such cases in those parts.

When I was on the Locust Control staff in the Rukwa Valley, I occupied a camp at a place called Kambo Ngombe.   My camp was situated in a small *vlei* where the grass never grew higher than 6 inches.   In this camp I kept three watch-dogs, who, for nights on end, made sleep quite impossible with their persistent barking.   In the background the howls of a hyena were always in evidence.   Frequently the dogs would rush out in pursuit of the prowler, and I feared that sooner or later they would be led into a trap and killed by the troublesome beast.

I determined to sit up one night and put an end to the trouble.   The dogs were securely tied up, and by midnight the din was once again in full swing.   Quite close to the camp

I could hear the hyena crunching bones. I soon had him lined up in the rays of a shooting torch, and was puzzled to see only one eye reflected in my light. Hyenas are the most difficult animals to hold in the rays of a light at night. They will rarely look at a light long enough to permit of careful aim. It was quite an hour later before I finally held the eye fully in the rays of my torch and accounted for the beast. Early the next morning I had the carcass dissected, and the stomach was found to contain part of the remains of a young native child. The most searching inquiries in the district brought no explanation. None of the natives in the neighbourhood knew of anyone who had lost a child in abnormal circumstances. The most likely explanation is that the child may have died from natural causes and was buried in a shallow grave from where it was dug up by the hyena.

Both cases I have mentioned here go to prove that the hyena will eat a human body if left within its reach, but it does not follow that he will kill human beings for food. The mystery of the one eye was explained by the fact that this hyena had at some time or other lost the other member either in a fight or as the result of a spear-wound inflicted by natives. I have often caught hyenas in drop-gate traps which I have set for lions, leopards, and cheetahs, and released in daylight. On these occasions I always carried a heavy hippo-hide sjambok with me, and as soon as they made for the opened gate I would treat them to one or more good lashes with the sjambok. On no occasion did any of them ever turn on me; their main concern was to get as far away from the scene as possible in the quickest time possible.

The other great scavenger of the bush, the vulture, likewise is not addicted to cannibalism. These repulsive-looking birds are for ever on the lookout for dead bodies, and will devour the largest carcasses in a matter of minutes. On the open plains it is never advisable to leave a dead animal unattended, and I frequently had great difficulty in protecting the carcasses of animals when several were killed in a small area and there were not sufficient guards to place at the kills. I finally hit on the plan of tying white flags to posts planted around kills. I often watched a hundred or more vultures gather round a carcass and approach within a few yards, when the slightest flutter of a flag would send them scattering back to what they considered a safe distance.

In one camp where jackals were very numerous and frequently raided the meat piles I shot quite a number. After the skins were removed the carcasses were left beneath a big tree where vultures gathered daily. This was a favourite spot with them, as offal and such other scraps were generally deposited there and devoured immediately by the ravenous birds. During the six months I spent in this camp some thirty jackal carcasses were dumped under the tree, but on no single occasion did the vultures pay the slightest attention to them. Any other scraps of meat left next to the jackals would be eagerly snapped up, but the jackal carcasses were left intact and had to be buried— much to the disgust of the natives, who felt that the vultures could easily have saved them the trouble of digging suitable pits. Whether it is a general rule for vultures to refuse the meat of a jackal I am not able to say. If it is not, the explanation in the present case may lie in the fact that natives in these parts frequently poisoned jackals to obtain the skins, which were of considerable value, and easily disposed of. It is quite possible that some vultures may have died as the result of eating poisoned carcasses, and this would explain their reluctance to eat the carcass of a jackal. In the case of lion, hyena, crocodile, snakes, and in fact any dead animal, the flesh was promptly and greedily devoured.

Another source of trouble in the Kambo Ngombe area during, and shortly after the rains, was the crocodile. These repulsive creatures generally lay in wait in river-beds where natives had to cross daily. During my stay in this camp I lost two native porters to the crocs. But later in the season, when the river had stopped flowing, it was quite a different story, and the natives amply avenged themselves on the saurians.

At several spots the sand-banks of the Rungwa River, which flowed only a few hundred yards past my camp, often exceeded 20 feet in height. One morning in September my attention was drawn by loud shouting and laughter in the direction of the river. On proceeding to the spot from where the disturbance came, I found that most of the 500 natives employed on Locust Control had gathered in the river-bed. At the moment of my arrival they had just managed to pull an

H

enormous croc from the sand-bank and were busy battering its skull in with pangas. For the rest of that day it was quite impossible to persuade them to go back to work. The entire length of the sand-bank was subjected to careful scrutiny, and wherever a tail protruded from the sand the croc was un-ceremoniously dragged from its retreat and beaten to death. During the course of one month no fewer than thirty-five crocs were accounted for in this manner. At that time crocodile-hunting had not yet become the profitable business it is today, and in only a few isolated cases were the skins removed by the natives for their own use.

Snakes also were a source of considerable danger in the Rukwa Valley at this time of the year, and cobras were especially numerous. It is now generally accepted that Africa was the original breeding ground of all cobras. For those who have only seen the usual 6- to 7-feet specimens, this theory may seem doubtful. In the Kambo Ngombe area, however, I frequently encounted specimens exceeding 9 feet in length. Once, on a particularly hot day, a native locust scout came in to report a herd of buffalo quite close to camp. Meat was always in short supply, and often scouts persuaded me to go after buffaloes which they claimed to have seen close by. As often as not, it meant long walks in the blistering sun without finding any trace of the reported animals.

On this occasion the scout was so emphatic that I finally decided I would go after the herd. He was told to take the lead, and I followed closely on his heels. We had walked only a short distance when he came to a sudden stop. For a moment I thought that he had spotted the buffaloes, but on looking ahead I found myself staring at the expanded hood of an enormous cobra. The head of the snake was level with that of the scout, who himself stood over 6 feet high. It was quite apparent that, allowing for only two-thirds of the reptile's body to be raised from the ground, this specimen would measure well over 9 feet in length. For fully ten seconds we stood motionless watching the expanded hood, then, shadow-like, it vanished from sight. There was a rustle in the grass, and we proceeded on our way. Unlike the King Cobra of India, African cobras are not naturally aggressive, and it is sound policy, when confronted with one of these reptiles, with expanded hood and swaying head to refrain from making any movement, for the slightest movement may be misconstrued and may result in an attack.

If that scout remained motionless when he looked into the eyes of the cobra, he showed no such tendencies a few minutes later when we came up with a herd of about twenty buffaloes, fast asleep under a big tree. We stalked them within 100 yards, and I picked out a large bull lying nearest to me. It often happens when a shot is fired on the open plains that the resulting echo will give an impression that it was fired in the opposite direction. It must have been this echo that prompted the herd to rush straight towards where we had taken cover under a cluster of bush. By the time I could break cover and take a bead on the bull in the lead, the distance separating us could not have been more than 50 yards. The next instant the herd swerved sharply to the left and made off at top speed. The entire incident occupied only about ten seconds, but when I looked for the scout he was well over 200 yards away, and still gaining speed. The outing was quite a profitable one, for in addition to the rare specimen of cobra I had seen, I had picked up two big bulls, and the camp was well supplied with meat for some days.

Later that night I had a visit from a snake expert who was engaged on scientific research in that area. When I mentioned to him that I had seen a cobra which I estimated to be more than 9 feet in length, my story was ridiculed. He was quite certain that no cobra of that length had ever been seen anywhere in Africa. I felt intensely annoyed that my story should be so summarily dismissed, and determined that I would make a special point of trying to collect the next specimen of unusual size, fully realizing that 10-feet cobras do not, as a rule, present themselves for collection in order to settle an argument. But any misgivings I may have had as to the prospects of my being able to collect a specimen to establish my claim were dispelled that same night, when my friend narrowly escaped being bitten by a snake.

The specie? A black cobra. The length? Nine feet 8 inches.

This event was given great prominence in the East African papers, and my friend lost no time in claiming all the available publicity for his remarkable discovery. When, some time later, I presented him with a specimen measuring 10 feet 2 inches, no mention of the fact was made in any newspaper. I have a sneaking suspicion that by the time he writes his memoirs of the Rift Valley campaign, this 10-feet 2-inch baby of mine will have been adopted.

Another lucky discovery which came my way during this campaign was that of a peculiar type of lizard ' unknown to science '. This strange reptile was definitely still in the transition stage between reptile and bird.

Measuring from 15 to 24 inches, there were only the smallest protuberances which served as legs. The method of locomotion was entirely snake-like. In fact, at this stage of its development the creature was predominantly snake. A notable exception was the complete absence of teeth. The capture and preservation of these strange creatures presented great difficulties, for the tail was so brittle that the merest touch would be sufficient to cause a complete rupture. Once again the news of this ' remarkable discovery ' was well and truly aired in the East African Press, with all the credit going to my fortunate friend. The manner in which the publicity of the discovery of this strange creature was handled so disgusted me that I have never troubled to find out how it was eventually classified.

During the rainy season at Kambo Ngombe camp, conditions finally became so bad that I had to remove my equipment. Snakes were the main source of worry. The valley was completely flooded and every dry spot was an asylum for snakes, scorpions, and other insects. On pitching camp on a small elevation one afternoon we started clearing a place for my tent. A big withered palm-tree had to be removed to make room for the natives and myself. As the natives began chopping down the palm there was a general exodus of scorpions; in a matter of minutes we killed no fewer than thirty-seven, and how many remained deep down in the ground I shall never know. My tent was erected in what I thought would be the safest spot, and I turned in early that night. Early next morning I decided to move to a better spot. On taking up my camp-bed I found seven young cobras comfortably installed under my ground-sheet. Just why they did not crawl into bed with me for warmth is anybody's guess.

CHAPTER XII

SNAKES—HARMLESS AND DEADLY

SINCE MY RETURN from Central Africa I have been surprised to see how deeply the average person is interested in snakes. Whenever I have discussed bush adventures I have invariably been asked how I managed to escape being swallowed, or bitten, by snakes; which I considered the most dangerous snakes in the bush, etc., etc.

When one takes into consideration the heavily populated areas in Africa where poisonous snakes are found daily, it is strange that there are so very few casualties resulting from snake-bites. I have no reliable statistics to refer to, but I think I am right in saying that, for every one casualty in Africa, where there is a much greater variety of poisonous snakes, there are at least twenty in India, and far and away the majority of casualties in India are caused by one specie— the Hamadryad, or king cobra, the world's most deadly reptile.

The most dangerous snake in Africa? It would be a bold person who would hazard an opinion on this subject. It depends on what exactly is meant by ' dangerous ' and also on the conditions applying when one falls victim to a bite from one of the recognized deadly snakes in that country. There can be little doubt that the puff-adder is responsible for far more fatal accidents there than any other snake, and he must consequently be considered the most dangerous of them all. But that does not mean that the poison of a puff-adder is more lethal than that of the mamba, cobra, or gaboon viper. The reason why the puff-adder is responsible for so many accidents is that it is a sluggish creature, incapable of rapid movement (excepting when it strikes), and has a tendency to coil up rather than attempt to escape if approached suddenly. If trodden upon whilst lying coiled up in a narrow pathway, a bite is certain to result.

Viewed from this angle, the puff-adder is more dangerous

than any other reptile. But as an effective killer, the puff-adder cannot compare with mamba, cobra, or gaboon viper. This is explained by the fact that puff-adder venom acts very slowly where human beings are concerned, and therefore allows more time for a victim to be treated after a bite. In the case of mamba or cobra, the poison acts very swiftly and death often supervenes in a very short time—depending on which part of the body the bite is inflicted. In the case of the gaboon viper—to my mind the most deadly snake in Africa—there is no cure against a full bite. The most highly concentrated antivenenes, prepared with puff-adder anavenom, have no neutralizing effects on gaboon viper venom, which, in addition to its hæmotoxic qualities, also contains powerful neurotoxic properties. In other words, it combines the lethal qualities of both mamba and puff-adder venom.

Like the puff-adder, the gaboon viper is also a sluggish creature, but unlike the puff-adder, its habitat is far more restricted. Like the puff-adder, it has enormous fangs, and can inject a much larger dose of poison at a single bite than any other snake in Africa. With a head often measuring over 4 inches wide and 5 inches long, and fangs more than 2 inches long, the gaboon viper is perhaps the world's most repulsive-looking reptile. Its appearance is not improved by the horn-like protuberances on its nose. But in spite of the deadly qualities of its venom, it is extremely rare for a gaboon viper to attack, and in all my years in the bush I never came across a single case of a gaboon viper bite.

Unfortunately this claim does not hold good where mambas, cobras, and puff-adders are concerned. It is only natural that I should have had many narrow escapes from snake-bites, but it only happened once that a snake actually struck at me—and fortunately missed me.

Out on the Usanga Plains in Tanganyika, where I was hunting at the time, I returned to camp late one afternoon to find the place in great turmoil. On a mat outside my tent door lay a native with wet cloths round his head and his hand heavily bandaged. On inquiring into the cause of the trouble, I was informed that the native in question was a victim of snake-bite. They had amputated the tip of his small finger where the snake had bitten him. After the accident they had killed the snake and had brought it along in a basket for me to examine. I did not trouble to examine it, but immediately injected a strong dose of antivenene serum, hoping that I would still be in time to save the man's life. It was only after I had injected the serum and tied a ligature above the wrist that I went over to examine the snake, which in this case proved to be a harmless grass snake, without poison ducts, and the fangs could have done little more than penetrate the skin. In view of the drastic precautions his friends had taken to save his life, it is perhaps as well that the bite was at the tip of a finger and not on an arm or leg.

Arriving at Kapili on Lake Tanganyika shortly before sunset one afternoon, I called on the native chief who lived not far from the European Guest House. Whereas natives generally keep a good clearance round their huts, I found in the chief's case that he had allowed the grass to grow to within a few feet of his hut. When I pointed out to him the risk of having snakes enter his home, he told me that he had lived there for more than fifteen years and had never seen a snake near the place. I remarked that he was lucky indeed and suggested that he did not tempt fate too far.

After some casual talk I returned to my camp to prepare for dinner. I had hardly sat down when a native runner came rushing up to inform me that shortly after I had left, the old chief had walked over to a friend's hut; on his way there, in the dim light, he had failed to notice a puff-adder lying coiled up in the narrow path. He had trodden on the snake and had suffered a bite in the leg just above the ankle. It was lucky for him that I was so close at hand and that I had the proper serum, which I immediately injected. The wound was cauterized and I applied a ligature above the knee, after which I returned to camp. Later that night I was called out again; the patient had taken a turn for the worse and it was feared he would die. I went down again and injected another dose of serum and remained with the old man for a couple of hours. His condition was extremely serious and I feared he would pass out before morning. But by sunrise he began to show signs of improvement, and, as in all cases of adder bite, once the poison is neutralized, recovery was fairly rapid. Three days later the victim was again able to walk about, but by that time the entire area for hundreds of yards round his hut had been cleared of every vestige of grass.

Up in northern Tanganyika, in the Kigoma area, I once came across a most sinister case of snake-bite. The area in which I was then hunting was controlled by an old chief who had made himself very unpopular with his people. The trouble in this case was that the chief was addicted to drink and *dagga* (hashish), and when under the influence, he became a positive menace to the rest of the population. I am a fluent Swahili linguist, and often at night, whilst lying in my tent, I listened to the hunting crowd as they sat talking round the camp-fire. On this particular night the conversation was devoted entirely to the misdeeds of the old chief.

Finally one of the natives, who must have taken all he could from the old man, predicted that within a day or two the chief would surely be killed by a snake. ' It is a pity we cannot rake up a cobra or a mamba, but the puff-adder will do,' I heard him say. It was definitely an intrigue in which I wanted to have no part, but as there had been considerable drinking, I passed the discussion off as so much wild talk, and gave it no further thought. But three days later I had ample reason to reflect on the discussion I had overheard.

The previous night the old chief, on returning from another wild spree, was bitten by a puff-adder. By the time he reached home he was already in a bad way, but he was still coherent, and told how a snake had suddenly reared up in front of him and struck twice in his leg as he was walking on the footpath. A few hours later he passed away—the victim of a puff-adder bite. He was buried the following day and the ' accident ' was accepted as perfectly normal. Had it not been for the conversation I had overheard I would have given the matter no further thought. I was fully five miles away from the chief's kraal, and could have done nothing to save him even had I been called on for help.

Somehow the set-up here was a bit too much to attribute to coincidence. I made discreet inquiries, but all I could get from the natives was that it was ' *shauri ya Mungu* '—the will of God. It was more than a month later, after I had left the district, that I got the full details from my old headman, Black, who had been with me for more than twenty years. That chief certainly died from puff-adder poisoning, but it was no accident. The puff-adder had been placed in the path with its tail nailed to a log of wood. The perpetrators of the crime had ingeniously contrived to nail the snake to the log, to which a thin strand of wire was tied. The log was pulled clear of the path, and any other passer-by was quite safe. It was when they heard the chief coming down on the path, singing at the top of his voice, that the log, with the snake nailed to it, was pulled directly in his way. By that time the snake had suffered hours of agony and must have been waiting anxiously to settle his score, and it was not surprising that two deep bites were inflicted in rapid succession. I did not think it was any part of my business to take the matter up. Often when returning late from a hunt I also walked those paths in the dark and—who knows?

At my camp at Kambo Ngombe in the Rift Valley, during the Locust campaign, the entire area was inundated owing to the heavy rains. Every spot not under water harboured snakes and insects of every description. I lived in daily fear of being bitten by poisonous snakes. One morning I left camp early to attend to a reported concentration of locusts in the valley. A native scout took the lead and walked in front of me on a narrow path. I was walking only a few yards behind him, and saw him make a sudden swerve from the path, but he was too late to avert the attack from a black mamba, and I saw the snake strike twice at his leg. Fortunately I was armed with a shotgun which I carried at the ready, and managed to kill the reptile before it could direct its attention to me.

The native was taken back to camp, a distance of about 200 yards, where I cauterized the wounds and injected serum. I sat talking to him for a couple of hours, and there were no visible ill effects; a little while later his breathing became troubled; after a further few minutes he jumped from his bed and grasped at his throat; in the next instant he pitched forward and fell on his face. Although the heart kept pumping for quite a minute after he had fallen, I firmly believe that he was dead by the time he hit the ground. Had we reversed the order of walking down that path that morning I should not be writing this now.

In Northern Rhodesia, very near to my camp, there was

quite a spate of accidents last year (1955), three of which unfortunately terminated fatally. In the first case a European
surveyor was bitten by a black mamba, and although large
doses of antivenene serum were injected almost immediately,
the victim died shortly after he was bitten. In this case a fang
had penetrated a vein, and the doctor who attended stated that
all the serum in Africa could not have saved the victim. The
strange feature of this case is that he survived long enough for a
doctor to be called. Usually, when snake venom, especially of
the neurotoxic type, is injected into a vein, death is almost
instantaneous.

In another case a youth, home for his school holidays, was
driving a tractor ploughing over a mealie land. In front of
the tractor was a small tree, only a few feet high, over which
the tractor was driven. But in the branches of the tree a black
mamba lay coiled up; as the tree was being pushed down the
mamba suddenly landed on the lap of the youth, and in rapid
succession inflicted no fewer than five bites. Thoroughly
alarmed, the victim ran home for help at top speed, and in so
doing he only aggravated the danger. In spite of prompt
medical treatment and numerous injections of serum, he died
a few hours later.

In the township of Lusaka I visited the enclosure of an old
Swahili ' snake man ' one morning. His collection consisted
of several species of cobras, puff-adders, night adders, boomslangs, and pythons, and these he handled with complete indifference. He showed me several scars on his hands where he
had previously been bitten by snakes. He claimed that he
was completely immune to all types of snake venom; in addition, he had a special ' muti ' which would cure any snake-bite.

On being asked whether his immunity also included the
mamba, he assured me that it did, and that he had actually
been bitten by a mamba. At that moment he had two black
mambas at home; only a week earlier a brood of baby mambas
were hatched and were doing very well—a fact of which he was
exceedingly proud. He promised me that on his next visit he
would bring the mambas with him and allow one to bite him
in my presence. But he did not have to wait for his next visit
to take a bite from the mamba; a few days later one of his pet
mambas attacked him, and in spite of his special *muti* and all the

medical profession could do for him, he died within twelve hours. He apparently had a certain immunity against snake-bites, for it is rare for a victim to survive a mamba bite for twelve hours in cases where serum is injected several hours after the accident, as it was in this case.

All three of the cases I have mentioned here happened within a period of six weeks. Shortly after this there was yet another case of snake poisoning in Lusaka. On this occasion a youth was bitten on the finger by a pet boomslang. Fool-ishly believing that the snake was not poisonous, he failed to have the bite attended to, but some hours later he began to show signs of acute poisoning. He was immediately rushed to hospital, where he lay in a critical condition for more than two weeks. During the whole of that period the wounds bled continuously, and it was only after twenty-one pints of blood had been transfused that he began to show signs of recovery. Accidents with boomslangs are extremely rare, and this is due to the fact that it is the least aggressive of all poisonous snakes. The fangs also are lodged so far back in the jaws that it is almost impossible for the reptile to secure a full bite. Al-though not comparable with the gaboon viper, boomslang venom contains a powerful combination of both hæmotoxic and neurotoxic poisons. It is one of the most deadly poisonous snakes in Africa.

So much for the poisonous snakes. Of the non-poisonous, the python is the most important and interesting. I once kept a python as a pet for more than two years. Pythons are harmless creatures when they have been tamed and can be very useful in camps where rats and mice are encountered. My association with the pet python came to an abrupt end one night when he had to be shot to prevent him from constricting me to death—but that was due to a little misunderstanding for which the python could hardly be blamed. A friend of mine was forced to spend a night in my camp owing to heavy rain. He had with him a small fox-terrier pup which crawled on to the camp stretcher on which I was sleeping that night.

I was awakened when the sides of the bed were being crushed against my body. The python certainly had no intention of doing me any harm, but he was after the pup. By the time I had awakened my friend with my screams, both the pup and I were already encircled in an iron grip. There is no way of inducing a python to release its strangle-hold, and the only thing to do was to shoot it. So there we are. The danger of an animal or reptile must be assessed on prevailing conditions. Normally that python was completely harmless, but once he had me in his coils he was every inch as dangerous as the most poisonous reptile—in fact more so, for a dose of serum would not be of any use to a man who has been constricted by a 14-feet python.

One does not as a rule turn to a snake to provide the fun of the fair in bush, but that happened once after I had had a successful day's hunting. The meat was carried back to camp, and that night a crowd of Mwembas were sitting round the camp-fire gorging themselves. Quite close to the fire was an enormous tree-trunk, hollow and decaying, on which some of the natives had seated themselves. By 9 p.m. I was comfortably installed in bed, when suddenly there was a wild commotion, with natives scattering in all directions and screaming at the top of their voices. For a moment I thought that a lion had suddenly appeared on the scene, and grabbing my rifle, I rushed out to deal with the trouble. The cause of the alarm, however, was nothing more serious than a python which had hibernated in the tree-trunk, and must have been awakened by the noise and the heat of the camp-fire. On leaving its nest it had crawled right in the midst of the circle where the blacks were sitting gorging themselves. It was with difficulty that I prevented them from killing the reptile and left it free to find its way out in the long grass.

CHAPTER XIII

NATURE RED

Just how mean can an animal get? In the case of the lion, I should imagine almost as mean as some human beings I have encountered. I was unfortunately not present to witness the entire episode I am about to describe, but as I came in at the dead end and saw all the evidence, there is no reason to disbelieve the story Black—my old headman and gun-bearer—told me when he returned to camp late one night.

Black had been privileged to sit up in a tree and watch an exhibition of meanness and vindictiveness which any cinematographer would have paid big money to film. Black, at that time, had been with me for more years than I care to remember, and had taken part in most of my big safaris. During all this period I had had many practical demonstrations of his amazing ability to scale the highest and most difficult trees in time of danger, in a manner that would leave any member of the ape family green with envy. Unlike any other natives I ever knew, Black was extremely fastidious about his feet, and would never think of going on a hunt without wearing a pair of outsize hobnail boots, which, normally, should have proved a great handicap to him when the necessity arose for him to look for safety in the tree-tops. In his case, however, the boots in no way impeded his movements; if anything, they seemed to help to accelerate his speed when danger threatened, and this did not apply only to his arboreal activities. With a buffalo on his trail, neither Landy nor Bannister would have had much on him over the first mile—boots notwithstanding.

Perhaps the finest exhibition of mass tree-climbing, with Black in the lead, came one morning when I was hunting buffalo on the Rungwa River in Tanganyika. We had picked up the trail of a herd shortly after sunrise, and stuck to it until just before noon, when the herd was spotted resting in the shade of a big tree. It was summer, and at that time of day heat mirages made visibility extremely difficult. But, as usual, the meat larder was empty, and in spite of the bad visibility, I determined to get as close to our quarry as possible and try my luck on the best target offering. When we had approached to within 200 yards of the herd, the animals must have picked up our scent, and they were quickly on their feet looking in our direction.

There was not much time for careful aim, and I took the animal nearest to me, which, owing to its size, I believed to be a bull. I had aimed for the heart, and the heavy thud as the bullet struck home convinced me that the shot was well placed. The herd immediately dashed off in an opposite direction, the wounded animal trailing well behind. As they swerved round in an open clearing, I observed that the wounded animal was not a bull, but an outsize cow. There was a heavy blood trail, which made it obvious that I had placed either a heart or a lung shot. If the former, the cow would be picked up within 100 yards or so, a lung shot might mean trailing her for a long distance, and in difficult country.

The tracks soon led into close shrub, and I was following the blood trail, which was clearly visible. Behind me was Black and twelve other native porters. The country was studded all over with tall thorn-trees, and the tracks led into even closer bush—so much so that had the wounded animal been a bull I would have abandoned the pursuit. But buffalo cows are not nearly as dangerous as the bulls, and it is rare for them to charge. I determined to stick to the trail, but Black and the other natives, believing the animal I had wounded to be a bull, now came to a stop and refused to go deeper into the close shrub.

When dealing with a wounded buffalo under such conditions it is always sound policy to get down flat and crawl, snake fashion, on the trail. A badly wounded buffalo on the defensive in close bush always stands with its head well raised, the idea apparently being that in this manner it can pick up any movement from a long distance. I immediately went down on my stomach and started crawling on the blood trail. I had gone barely 20 yards when there was a vicious snort just ahead of me. The cow had gone to ground, and had spotted me crawling up to her. She was by now so weakened by the loss of blood that she made no attempt to rise, and I quickly placed a brain shot. From the time of the snorting to the time I had shot the cow not much more than ten seconds could have elapsed. But in those few seconds the entire retinue of porters, with Black in the lead, were already negotiating the highest branches of the surrounding trees. I have mentioned this incident to illustrate Black's amazing ability to make practical use of a suitable tree when occasion demanded it, as it did on the occasion I am about to describe.

On the morning of the lion incident I was not feeling too well, and had sent Black out to try to shoot something for the pot. For this purpose I had given him a 9.3-mm. rifle, and as he left camp shortly before sunrise, I expected him back by 9 a.m. at the latest—game being quite plentiful in the vicinity. By sunset that afternoon Black had not returned, and I had already fired two shots to give him direction, in case he had lost his way. It was close on 9 p.m. before he finally put in an appearance. For the whole of that day he had sat high up in the branches of a tree and watched the sequence of events which he now described to me.

A couple of hours or so after he left camp that morning he had come on a pride of lions—male, female, and two cubs. An indifferent shot at the best of times, Black had stalked the lions until he got to the base of a large tree; from this advantageous position he had fired at the lion, aiming for the neck. But the shot was badly placed and, instead of killing the animal instantly, he had fractured the spinal column far back above the hind quarters. There was a terrific roar, which in itself would have been sufficient to send Black up into the treetops, but when the lioness came for him in full charge the situation was aggravated; he promptly discarded the rifle, and by the time she reached the base of the tree Black was already comfortably installed on one of the higher branches, well out of her reach. Time is always a nebulous factor where natives are concerned, but Black maintained that the lioness kept circling that tree for fully two hours; all this while the lion, incapable of displacing itself, was creating a fearful din.

' The very earth was shaking with his roars,' Black declared.

Finally, convinced that there was nothing to be gained by circling the tree, the lioness had returned to her mate—perhaps with the intention of offering him her sympathy, but the lion was in no mood for such an advance, and the moment she rubbed against him and put out her paw in a playful gesture, he struck out a vicious blow with his front paw. The lioness was knocked down, and before she could gain her feet she was subjected to a violent attack and suffered a terrific mauling. It was with great difficulty that she finally managed to crawl beyond his reach. For several hours she lay groaning and grunting, with blood flowing from the deep wounds the lion had inflicted with his fangs. By five o'clock that afternoon the groaning ceased and the lioness rolled over dead.

Black was just about to start descending the tree when there was yet another vicious snarl. One of the cubs had approached the lion too closely, and in so doing had paid the same price as the mother had done earlier in the day. The cub was killed outright with a terrific stroke of one of the front paws. With this exhibition of meanness and vindictiveness, occasioned no doubt by the pain he was suffering, one would have thought the brute had spent his fury. But that monster still had plenty of spite left in his crippled body. Shortly after the cub had been killed he once again turned on the carcass and promptly started to tear it to pieces. For some moments Black believed that the proceedings were nothing worse than a fiendish exhibition of pent-up fury, and sat watching. But much worse was to follow. A few minutes later the brute was once again back on the carcass of the cub. This time he was not content only to tear it apart, but he was actually devouring it piece by piece. With the lioness out of the way and the lion incapable of pursuing him, Black descended the tree, retrieved the rifle, and put an end to the vindictive beast.

It was too late to go out that night and verify the story Black had told me, but early next morning we were on the scene. All the evidence was there to support Black's story. We collected the hides of the two adults and immediately started scouring the country in search of the other cub. Despite an hour's careful search we failed to find any trace of him, and returned to camp. In all my experience in the bush I consider this the worst exhibition of meanness and vindictiveness I have ever come across.

On a number of other occasions I have watched terrific battles between males of the different species of animals, and the nearest approach to this exhibition of vindictiveness came from a hippo bull. This incident also happened on the Rungwa River, where I was then hunting. The river, at this time of the year, had all but stopped flowing, but there were several very large pools which small schools of hippo frequented regularly. In one of these the hippos were so tame that they would approach within 10 yards and stand and look at one in wonder. I often went to this pool and watched the antics of a large family. They were in no way put out by my presence and I often sat for an hour or more admiring them. Usually there was a lot of frolicking and mock fights between the younger members. But one morning when I arrived on the scene a crowd of natives had gathered on the banks of the river. High up on the opposite bank two hippo bulls were engaged in a life-and-death struggle. I sat watching the battle for more than half an hour before one bull was battered to the ground, where he was subjected to a savage attack. Every now and again the victor would retreat for several yards and make a headlong rush at his stricken opponent and bury his tusks deep in the sides and stomach. When finally the victor had satisfied himself that his opponent was quite dead, he rejoined the other members who had been watching the struggle intently from the pool. But in that brute brain vengeance still burned deeply, for on three more occasions he left the pool to attack the carcass of his vanquished foe.

The next day I again visited the pool. Everything was quiet and peaceful. The dead hippo was still lying where it had fallen the previous day. I was surprised to see that the meat had not been taken by the natives from the nearby village. The explanation lay in the fact that the hippo was killed out of water. Had he been killed in the water he would have been considered as belonging to the fish family; being killed out of water made him a pig. They were all Swahilis of the Mohammedan faith. Mohammedans will eat fish, but their religion forbids them to eat a pig.

On yet another occasion I witnessed a fight which I fully expected to produce many thrills, but it ended as tamely as a boxing match with a disqualification in the first round. On this occasion I was sitting behind a rock high up on the banks of the Sira River, waiting for a monster-size croc to come to

I

surface from a deep pool. I had been waiting patiently for more than two hours without any sign of the croc, when unexpectedly a young buffalo bull came to drink. I was still busy lining the buffalo up carefully in my sights when suddenly there was a terrific commotion at the side of the pool. The croc had apparently been lying submerged under water all the time I had been waiting for it to surface, with only its nose exposed.

The moment the buffalo had started drinking he had gone into action and seized it by the nose. In an instant the buffalo reared up on its hind legs and began pulling frantically to escape from the iron grip. On two occasions fully half of the croc was dragged from the water, but slowly it gained the upper hand, and finally the buffalo's head was pulled deep down into the water. The entire business did not last more than five minutes. In a short time the croc, apparently satisfied that there was no more fight left in the buffalo, came to surface. That was exactly what I had been waiting for all morning, and a well-placed shot in the head with a heavy .404 calibre rifle brought the day's excitement to an end. When the carcass was eventually dragged from the water I was not surprised that this monster croc had so effectively mastered a 500-lb. buffalo, for the measurement from tip to tip showed that this brute was only a few inches under 17 feet in length.

I had come to the pool in response to the appeal from the native headman at the nearby village. At that time the croc had already accounted for no fewer than five natives. The last victim, a woman, had been taken only two days before I arrived on the scene. On dissecting the carcass I found no human parts, but the stomach contained a collection of native beads and four bracelets. If this was the same brute that was responsible for the last tragedy, the body must have been completely digested, or hidden somewhere in the dense reeds, which probably was the case, as the croc has a marked preference for putrid flesh.

Of all the denizens of the forest, the croc, to my mind, is by far the most repulsive. The most poisonous reptiles never fail to arouse my interest, and I never let an opportunity pass of studying them—even after they have been killed, but the croc stirs only one emotion in me, and that is one of revulsion.

Photo: *W. F. Schack, National Parks Board, Pretoria*

Giraffe in natural habitat

Photo: Major Harrison Lusaka

Leopard tortoise—a great delicacy amongst certain natives

Photo: Major Harrison Lusaka

Young bush buck—amongst the most graceful of smaller animals

Weight for weight perhaps the leopard is the most deadly killer of all. Seen here on the defensive

Photo: Major Harrison Lusaka

Photo: Major Harrison Lusaka

Leopard on the alert

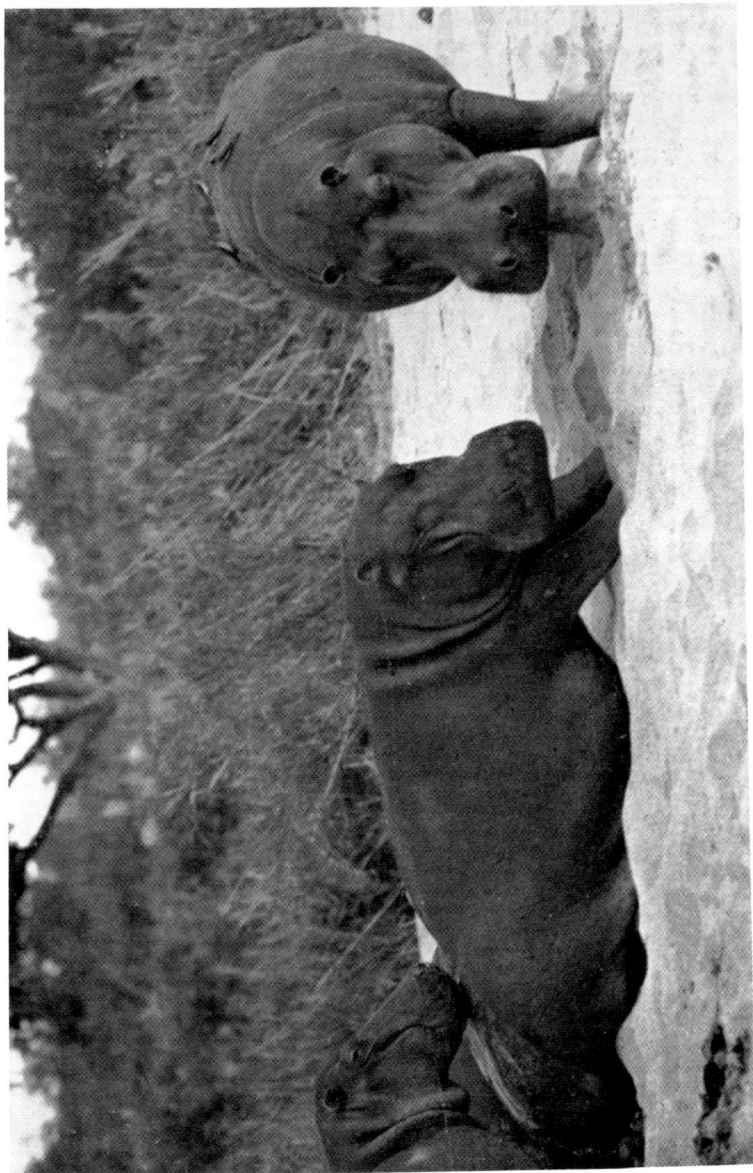

"One morning we will wake up and find ourselves dead"

Photo: W. F. Schack, National Parks Board, Pretoria

"I had a magnificent bull lined up in my sights at close range"

Church built by the White Fathers along Lake Tanganyika

Doris in pensive mood

The picture on the wall

(See chapter 23)

Still another one-sided fight I witnessed, and which lasted a shorter time than it will take me to describe, was when a python fastened itself on to the trunk of an elephant bull. Earlier on I had relinquished my interest in the elephant, on realizing that the tusks would not weigh more than 30 lb. each. I had been sitting high up in the branches of a nearby tree all that morning, watching an elephant path. The bull had put in a belated appearance, and finally came to a stop under a tree quite close to me. Just what led to the python assuming the role of aggressor I do not know, but the first intimation I had of something unusual happening was when the bull squealed loudly and stretched its ears wide. For a moment I thought he had spotted me in the branches of the tree where I was sitting and that he was going to try to dislodge me from my perch. It was only then that I noticed the trunk raised high over its head with the snake dangling from it.

The next instant the python was dashed to the ground with terrific force, and just to make sure that the job was effectively done, the elephant proceeded to trample the snake into the ground under its massive feet. I fired a shot over the head of the bull, and he immediately set off at a fast pace. A few minutes later I descended the tree and proceeded to the spot. That snake was truly and effectively killed—in fact it had been trodden into a complete pulp. I have in this case assumed that the python was the aggressor in the first place. The position I occupied in the tree some distance away and the unexpectedness of it all made it impossible for me to observe accurately just what it was that had roused the elephant's ire. It is, of course, possible that he approached the python too closely, and that it reared up its head in an offensive gesture. This may have led the bull to believe that the snake was about to attack, and would explain his subsequent action.

Of the larger antelopes, the sable and roan are the two species that most frequently fight to the death. On one occasion I came across a dead sable bull. It was obvious that he had fallen victim to the horns of another bull. A few hundred yards away I came upon the dead body of the second bull; he could not have survived the battle for long. In the distance was the herd, grazing peacefully. Duels to death generally have their origin in the pursuit of a female. If the female in

that herd who was responsible for the trouble had any knowledge of the damage she had caused, she certainly showed no
signs of conscience.   But, then, it is a feminine prerogative, in
the society of both man and beast, to have the males fight to
death for her favours.   The stupidity lies with the males in
allowing their feelings to take them to such lengths.

Looking through a pair of powerful binoculars on another
occasion, I watched two sable bulls fighting.   The battle
lasted for fully half an hour before the one bull was killed;
the other was so badly injured that he barely managed to limp
away from the scene of battle.   When I caught up with him he
was lying prostrate, with blood oozing from both nostrils.   A
timely bullet saved him from slowly bleeding to death from
serious lung injuries.   Koodoos, the most elegant of the large
antelopes, also frequently figure in death duels, but their
enormous horns often prove a serious handicap in such encounters.   I once came across two dead bulls.   During the
struggle their horns had become so entangled that they were
unable to extricate themselves.   Up to that time neither bull
had inflicted a serious injury and both must have died from
hunger or during their struggle to free themselves.

Perhaps I was unlucky on the two occasions I saw fights
between buffalo bulls.   To my mind, the most deadly vindictive killer of them all where human beings are concerned,
the buffalo shows none of that vindictiveness in a fight for
supremacy with other herd bulls.   The two fights I witnessed
were both half-hearted affairs and did not last long.   In both
cases I bagged one of the contenders, but apart from a few
superficial wounds, there was nothing to indicate that serious
damage had been done.

Yes, it is true, nature is red in tooth and claw, and on every
side we see battles for the survival of the fittest.   But there is
at least one exception that does not conform with this scheme
of nature.   The eland, the world's largest antelope, with bulk,
weight, and horns ideally adapted for offence as well as defence, is yet the most inoffensive of beasts.   Every other
creature, from the ant to the elephant, will fight for its life, its
love, and its existence, but the eland disdains such practice.   I
have never come across a case of two eland bulls fighting for
superiority.   Mortally wounded, a bull will lie down and die,

and even if approached in this condition, he will make no effort to defend himself. It is for this reason that I have never killed an eland unless extreme necessity demanded it, and even then I have always been reluctant to eat the meat of this harmless, inoffensive creature.

CHAPTER XIV

MY PETS AND I

WILD ANIMALS, BRED in captivity, can generally be tamed very easily, and make delightful pets, but it has always surprised me to see how easily young ones captured in the bush can be tamed, and the great affection they then show for human beings. At different times I have raised almost every species of animal to be found in Central Africa—elephants, rhinos, and giraffes being the notable exceptions—but my collection did include buffalo, hippo, lion, leopard: just about all of the antelope family, most of the apes—including the chimp, gorilla, and, for good measure, harmless or non-venomous snakes, and even the latter made good and useful pets.

A buffalo calf, whose mother came within inches of killing me, lived for two months, by which time he followed me wherever I went. A young hippo whose mother had pushed him into a pit trap from which we extricated him with great difficulty became so troublesome and costly to keep that after six months I decided to get rid of him. By the time we parted company he had also reached the stage where he followed me like a dog.

A chimp which I had kept for two years became addicted to alcohol. When I carelessly left my provisions case unlocked one afternoon, he got hold of a bottle of Cooper's Dip, which he mistook for whisky. Just how much he swallowed before he discovered his mistake, I do not know, but in less than an hour he lay dead outside my tent door. I had become so fond of that chimp, and he had provided me with so much pleasure, that his death affected me as greatly as the loss of a child would have done.

By and large, it is only the fact that the chimp is unable to speak that distinguishes him from a child in the matter of intelligence. Jacko could do almost anything but talk. When I sat writing I usually handed him a pad and pencil, and he ' wrote ' as fast as I did. The only difference was that some of my writing was legible, Jacko's consisted mainly of vertical and cross lines. At food time his place was always reserved next to me. His behaviour in general was good when the usual everyday fare appeared on the menu, but when there was fruit, sweets, or such-like titbits, he had to be restrained.

Although he was born in the bush and captured when he was several months old, he was never very fond of walking. Usually he followed me into the bush for a mile or so and then went through all the movements to show me that he was tired and had had enough of it. He always found his way back to camp on his own, where he would welcome my return—often late at night. Following bush manners whilst on safari, he was always given his share of dry grass and a blanket or two at night. Jacko put far more time into preparing his bed and making it comfortable than I ever did. Often he would get out of bed three or four times to straighten out a bump or twig that disturbed him. At sundowner time he was always in evidence, and his manners then were distinctly bad. If a drink was ever left unattended on a chair or table beside me, he would quickly snatch it and gulp it down. When Jacko was ' under the influence ' his antics were screamingly funny, but he strongly resented any laughter at his expense and would often retaliate in chimp language which I did not understand. His loss left me disconsolate for many months.

A baby gorilla which we captured up in the Kivu lived for only a week. In spite of the close affinity these anthropoids bear to the human family, this baby refused to make friends, and repulsed all advances in that direction—even refusing to take food or milk. He must have been his father's favourite son, for after we had captured him the entire family menaced us for several minutes. It was when the old male bared his fangs and started beating his enormous chest that I had to fire several warning shots over his head. That male stood a full 6 feet high and I should have hated him to embrace me. Had I known at the time that baby gorillas are so difficult to raise, I would have given him back his son and left them to go their way.

Apart from the chimp, leopards were my favourite pets. For more than twenty years I was never without one; most of them I kept for over five years, and I never experienced a moment's trouble or anxiety on their account. Elsewhere I have given a full description of how I once used one as a watch-dog and how he settled the score with a persistent burglar. In spite of their unsavoury reputation, they are animals capable of showing great affection. They are very playful—even when grown up—and are spotlessly clean in their habits. For some reason, all five of my leopards intensely disliked children, and as soon as a child appeared near their cage they became agitated and restive.

When I was operating a small gold-mine in Tanganyika I built an enormous cage, which I covered in with chicken wire; old tree-trunks and branches were placed inside, and when I stopped collecting I had twenty-seven vervet monkeys inside it. They are the most amusing creatures to watch. Like human beings, they soon elect—or accept—a leader. The boss of this lot was an old female with the haughtiest manner I ever saw on any ape. When the main meal of the day, which usually consisted of mealie-meal mixed with honey or milk and sugar, was served in a huge dish, she would majestically descend from her perch and take her fill. On no account would she allow a single member of the family to join her at her meal. Whilst she was feeding all the other twenty-six members of the family sat in a circle and waited until she had satisfied herself, after which she would return to her perch and watch the other members gorging themselves and fighting for position.

It often happened that I threw a handful of sweets or nuts into the cage, for which there would be a wild scramble. Such titbits were immediately pushed into the pouches in their cheeks. If it ever happened that the old girl failed to collect her share, she would grab a lucky possessor by the neck, push his head down on the ground, and dig the sweet out of the pouch with her forefinger.

'Fleaing' time in the afternoons provided the greatest amusement. They systematically took turns in giving each other a thorough going over from head to foot. It is generally believed that they rid each other of fleas and ticks, but I do not believe that this is actually the case. The round ball formation of the fingers and short thumb would make it extremely difficult, if not impossible, to grip such small insects. What they actually do is to scratch scabs from the skin.   These have a small salt content which is relished.

When kept in the manner I have described, the vervet is an amusing and interesting pet, but they do not take kindly to being handled when full-grown.   They are, in fact, extremely dangerous creatures, being intensely nervous and highly strung.   They will bite on the least provocation, and more so when they are unexpectedly scared or deprived of a delicacy.

At one time I kept a mixed assortment of pets, consisting of dogs, cats, leopards, monkeys, baboons, and a mongoose.   The country all round was infested with leopards, and the entire collection of pets was put into a large cage at night for safety. When the door was opened in the mornings a half-bred Alsatian bitch was always the first to emerge.   Once outside the cage she would stand in the doorway and let the others out, one at a time.   For some reason she determined that the leopard should always be the last to leave the cage.   If ever he tried to force his way out ahead of the others she would fly at him; the leopard would immediately turn over on his back with all four paws stretched upwards whilst she stood snarling over him until she decided it was time for him to leave.   But as the leopard grew older he became less docile, and one morning when the bitch again flew at him he subjected her to a terrific mauling.   After that Spots was kept in an open cage at night.

One night one of the vervet escaped and could not be recaptured; later on he must have decided to join his old friend Spots and spend the night with him.   When we awoke the next morning only two small pieces of the vervet's hind legs were found in the cage.   The friendship had ended up on a bad note.

The dog-face (Chacma) baboon, in spite of its repugnant appearance, I found to be one of the best and most intelligent pets.   I kept a family of three—father, mother, and daughter— and they all became very devoted to me.   Bobby, the father, was an extremely intelligent ape, and readily took to beer; which he could consume in large quantities.   But, unlike the chimp, he had no use for strong alcoholic beverages.   One afternoon, as a special treat, I gave him a big helping of Avocat (home brewed).   With its rich sugar and egg content

I expected Bob to go for it in a big way. The first mouthful went down with apparent relish, but suddenly he stopped, wiped his mouth, and gave me a scathing look. The next instant he picked up the dish and threw it straight at my face. Bob objected to the excessive alcohol content!

One afternoon I sat watching the three of them playing. Suddenly there was loud screeching and chattering. The cause of the alarm was an enormous black cobra which had suddenly appeared on the scene. I quickly rushed indoors for a shotgun, but by the time I came out the tail of the snake was disappearing into a deep hole near by. I did not like the idea of having such a dangerous reptile so close to the house, and decided to dig it out and destroy it. Whilst the digging was in process, the three apes sat chattering loudly.

After considerable digging and shovelling, and just as I scooped up a spadeful of earth, the cobra streaked out of the hole at a terrific speed. I was so taken aback that I stumbled and fell in my efforts to avoid the snake. The next moment both Bob and Sylvia, the mother, had jumped on my chest. I fully expected them to tear me to pieces, in their nervous and alarmed state. But instead the pair of them clung on to me tightly. When I finally got to my feet the snake had disappeared into the long grass. I have often wondered whether those two apes jumped on to my chest with an idea of protecting me against the snake?

It was quite a year later that I left on my big safari in the Rift Valley. It was not convenient to take three baboons on such a trip, and when I reached a large mango grove with a fresh-water spring near it I decided to set them free. They were taken deep into the grove and their collars removed. None of them showed any eagerness to take to the trees, and sat looking at me. Thinking that they did not realize that they were free, I pushed Bob forward with my foot. He had never been harshly treated, and took offence at being pushed in this manner. He immediately flew at me and fastened his fangs in my arm. The bite was not very serious and he was soon pacified. After that I returned to the truck, thinking that they would take advantage of their liberty and raid the plantation. But I was mistaken; when I reached the truck all three were following close behind me. I quickly started the motor and set off at top speed. For fully a mile the three of them followed the truck, until they were finally tired out.

During the next three months I received regular reports from natives that each time a car or truck passed the plantation all three baboons would rush to the roadside, hoping to find me there. I was deeply touched by that, and more so when it eventually turned out that I could easily have taken them with me. The conditions were not nearly as difficult as I had anticipated. When I returned from my safari some months later, the natives from a nearby village told me that one morning as a car approached the plantation the baboons again rushed to the road to investigate. The driver pulled up and shot both Bob and Sylvia. The little one clung to its dead mother and was captured. I can only hope that that valiant ' sportsman ' will atone for his ruthless act and treat little Julie well.

The last leopard I had also came to a sad end. When he broke loose from his chain one night another valiant sportsman who knew that it was a tame animal promptly filled him up with lead as he walked past his house. The mongoose who was expected to rid the house of snakes proved to be a complete failure. Certain species of mongoose are terrified of a snake, and when one morning I tossed a dead snake into his cage he became hysterical and nearly died from fear. A harmless live grass snake had a similar effect upon him. He did not seem happy in captivity, so I set him free, and although he returned to the house on a few occasions at first, he finally disappeared.

One of the sweetest little pets I ever had was a young Silver Jackal, but, like all jackals, he turned out to be an incorrigible thief. Nothing edible, from a pot of jam to a joint of roast beef, could be left on the table unattended when Jackie was about. In the end all the dogs copied his thieving habits. If ever Jackie was caught in the act of stealing he would immediately turn over on his back and stretch out all four paws upwards and hope for the best. Jackie came to grief when he raided a native chicken run for the umpteenth time and had a spear put into him.

The last of my favoured pets was an amazing parrot who never tired of shouting at the natives—most of whose names he knew. They were regularly subjected to a tongue-lashing if they came too near the house—a bad habit he had learned from me. When Doris played the piano he usually sat beside her whistling and singing loudly. Polly was a Drdla fan, and could sing a few bars from both the 'Serenade' and the 'Souvenir'—the latter with great emphasis. 'You make me sick', he usually shouted when someone upset him—an expression Doris frequently used when the houseboys annoyed her.

When the dogs' food was put out Polly immediately took possession and kept them away until he had had his fill. They all feared that wicked beak. A Pointer pup who resented being driven away from his food, but who had fallen foul of the beak on several occasions previously, generally stood near the dish, flapping his ears and barking loudly. Polly would sit and watch him with a look of disgust. When the barking became too noisy and annoyed him, he would call out 'Voetsak, you skunk'—another expression he learned from me.

Before I bought Polly he must have belonged to an old prospector or hunter who suffered from asthma or T.B., for when Polly went into a fit of coughing he gave one the impression that death was absolutely imminent. After the spell of coughing was over he would clean his throat in a most disgusting manner and spit loudly. A long-drawn-out sigh indicated that the attack was over. When he burst into loud laughter, only the deaf and dumb could refrain from joining in. Parrots are said to live to an age of a hundred years sometimes, but when they fall ill they generally die in as many minutes. My Polly gave us a great entertainment one Christmas Eve, but our Christmas was completely wrecked when I found him dead outside my bedroom door the next morning. Doris was deeply distressed and wept bitterly; in passing she said to me, 'It is the inevitable destiny that awaits us all; I wonder whose turn it will be next.' Little did we know that she herself was destined to fill the role a few months later.

Antelopes provided little else but gracefulness and beauty around the camp. When young, they will generally follow one everywhere, but they soon respond to the call of the wilds and return to their natural haunts. But there was one antelope, an old Topi cow, who, if she never filled the role of a pet, nevertheless became a great favourite of the family. One morning whilst Doris and I sat at breakfast in the Great Rift Valley, she suddenly appeared near our tent. Close on her heels followed a few-months-old calf. They stood looking at our tent for several minutes and then walked quietly off.

For the next two months she appeared almost daily— always with the calf at her heels. On the few occasions when she failed to put in an appearance we were always worried, and feared that something untoward might have happened to her and her baby. There were many occasions when the meat larder was completely empty and a piece of Topi steak would have filled the gap admirably, but mother Topi and her baby were perfectly safe. The natives, who were often as meat hungry as ourselves, could never understand such a procedure, and less so when they were all warned that our visitors were not to be molested in any circumstances whatever. The situation was aggravated in their minds when frequently they had to walk 20 or more miles with me in search of game and returned empty-handed.

A fortnight before we were due to leave the camp I started firing shots over the Topi's head whenever she appeared on the scene. By the time we finally left she had not put in an appearance for nearly a week. If she has been able to survive the dangers that threaten all antelopes in the bush, the baby should long ago have reached the age of maturity and mother Topi should now be enjoying the middle-age spread. Let us hope this is so.

Pets often made life pleasant and more bearable in lonely places, and brought me much happiness; but I have long since given up raising them. Sooner or later comes the time to part with them, and losing them always brings sorrow and sadness.

CHAPTER XV

HUNTERS—GOOD AND BAD

Arriving back in my camp late one afternoon, far down in the Usanga Plains where I had established a depot for maize supplies for a mining company with whom I was associated at the time, I found a native messenger waiting for me with a letter. The letter was from the mine manager advising me that a personal friend of his would call on me the following Saturday and asked me to take him out and show him as much game as possible during his short stay.

The manager, himself, was not a hunter, and was not aware of the fact that at that time of the year, December, conditions in the field were totally against hunting and that it was practically impossible to see game at all owing to the long grass which, for the greater part, grew to more than 10 feet high in the plain.

My camp was well off the beaten track, and owing to the bad road conditions my food supplies were at a very low ebb. Game meat always filled the gap admirably. But owing to the prevailing conditions I rarely went out to hunt, for it was only occasionally that I could use my light truck to take me the 15 miles to good hunting country. Walking in a temperature of 120 deg. in the shade held very little appeal for me and for that reason even this source of supplies was seriously reduced. My visitor would be in for a very lean time as far as food was concerned, but there was nothing I could do to alter the arrangements in time, and the best I could hope for was that the weather would relent and that the roads would improve sufficiently for one or two outings.

As usual, I had with me a full complement of rifles to suit any type of hunting I might have to resort to in order to keep the pot boiling and in this way I hoped to make my guest's visit as pleasant as possible. That Saturday night I sat up until late waiting for him, but he failed to put in an appearance. The next day I was out in the field until late and when I got back to camp it was to find him comfortably installed in my tent. The visitor was a consulting engineer from South Africa and had apparently done a considerable amount of hunting previously. He was an enormous man, standing well over 6 feet and weighing a full 300 lb.

After the customary courtesies the conversation drifted to hunting and the newcomer was greatly interested in my collection of guns. He himself was armed with a .303 Service Rifle and before the evening closed it was decided that we would go out on the trail of any worth-while animal early the following morning. The weather had fortunately eased up and it would be possible to use a light truck for part of the way. Even at this early stage of the conversation it was apparent that the new-comer was full of bombast and eager to tell of his many adventures. He was particularly anxious to hunt buffaloes, and inquired into the possibilities of getting a record-size pair of horns.

Only the week before I had survived two of the most nerve-wracking experiences of my life with wounded buffaloes. In one of these one of my trackers had been tossed and badly mauled by a wounded bull before I could come to his rescue. With the light .303 rifle my visitor had, I did not think he was well equipped for a buffalo hunt, but I did not bother to tell him this, nor of the two adventures the previous week. One can get a lot of fun out of this type of 'know-all' in the bush, and I decided to play the innocent.

It was not long before my guest was giving me a detailed account of some of his most sensational exploits with game in the bush. Elephant, buffalo, rhino, lion, and leopard—to this famous Nimrod they all looked alike, and the most stirring account I listened to that night was of the occasion on which he had dropped five buffaloes with as many shots, as they were running away from him. A casual inquiry elicited the information that his shooting was so deadly on this occasion that a light-6.5 mm. rifle had sufficed to bring about such an astonishing result. On going over the details, he had to agree with me that in the circumstance the last buffalo was brought down at a range of nearly 500 yards.

'A well-placed neck shot will bring them down every time,' he informed me.

I did not think it worth while to tell him that only a few months before I had sat on an open truck which was unexpectedly charged by a bull and that I had seen five bullets from a 6.5-mm. rifle placed into its skull and neck at point-blank range, and all the bull did was to shake its head. When we finally retired for the night I had had a fill of the most blatant lies and exaggerations I had ever listened to. It had also been arranged that we would go out early the next morning in search of buffalo or any other game in the offing.

At sunrise the next day we set out in a light truck in a direction where I knew buffaloes could be found near a water-pool in the early mornings. My guest had an ample supply of ammunition for his .303, but my supplies for all calibres had dwindled very seriously during the past two months. Although I had only a few rounds left for my heavy .404 rifle, I decided to stick to the heavier gun for the occasion, as, in spite of the wild talk I had listened to the night before, I did not have much faith in my companion in the event of trouble.

Less than half an hour after we had left camp we put up a pride of lions—male and female. The range was a little over 200 yards, but, as they were already showing signs of nervousness, I suggested that Gert (for the purpose of this story) should try for the female, whilst I took a chance at the male. Almost simultaneously two shots rang out, and the male went down after it had run a short distance. The female made a leap high into the air as the bullet struck close to her and immediately took off at a fast pace. Our two next shots brought no results, and she disappeared in long grass. Gert was highly excited, and insisted that we should follow the lioness, whose leap into the air he attributed to a hit. We drove up to the male, where I posted a couple of white flags to protect the carcass from vultures, and from there we set off on foot on the trail of the lioness.

When, after an hour of close trailing, there was still no sign of her, I suggested that we abandon the trail and go after buffalo instead. For a while we walked in fairly open country on the trail of a small herd which had passed earlier in the morning, but now the tracks led into close country and high grass. I thought it would be a good idea before going farther, to explain to Gert just how dangerous buffaloes can be in such country, and cautioned him to exercise the greatest care and keep his rifle at the ready, at the same time to maintain a distance of not less than 20 yards between us, in case of a sudden charge from close quarters.

I had intentionally exaggerated the danger for his benefit, but, as I felt reasonably certain there were no wounded or lone bulls in the neighbourhood, I did not anticipate any trouble. Watching Gert's face as I spoke to him, I could see that he had very little enthusiasm for the job, and when he inquired as to which would be the best place to shoot for in case of a charge, I curtly replied, 'Just shoot him in the neck—the same as you did the other five you told me about last night.'

For a short distance Gert kept the prescribed distance of twenty paces between us, but now, as we were entering taller grass, I found him walking right beside me. I was still signalling for him to move farther out to his left when there was a loud rustle in the grass right in front of us. The next instant Gert had flung both his arms round my neck, and with his twenty stone of weight on top of me, we both went sprawling to the ground. But for the fact that the cause of the alarm was a bushbuck which had gone to sleep in the tall grass, this foolish escapade might have ended in tragedy. In explanation of his peculiar behaviour, Gert was soon telling me that he had never hunted buffalo in this kind of country previously. His stature as a hunter, compared with his bravado of the previous night, had undergone a remarkable change, and he lost no time in accepting my proposition that we abandon the trail of the buffaloes and return to the spot where we had left the lion.

Trailing the lioness, and the fruitless pursuit of the buffalo herd, had taken fully four hours, and it was another hour or more before we got back to where the lion lay. By that time the stomach was enormously distended, and I decided to have one more good joke at the expense of my bombastic hunting companion. I suggested that he sat down next to the carcass whilst I took up my position behind him. In this position of honour, a native scout would photograph the tableau. The long walk earlier in the day had so utterly fatigued Gert that it took him quite a time to get his huge frame comfortably settled beside the carcass. I waited until he had struck what he believed was a dignified pose, with rifle in hand, and as he gave the

K

signal for the snap to be taken I jumped on the bloated stomach with my full force. There was a loud grunt as the gasses were expelled as a result of the impact. But before the grunting had terminated, Gert, with his twenty stone of bulk, was literally flying through space, screaming for help at the top of his voice. ' Shoot him in the neck ! ' I shouted after him, but Gert had already broken through the sound barrier and did not hear me. When eventually he thought it safe to look back over his shoulder, it was to see me sitting comfortably on the carcass.

That night we again sat round the camp-fire and talked hunting. Gert had no more hair-raising stories to tell me, but I thought it was a good moment to inform him that I had come on this safari in order to collect more material for a book I was then writing on my thirty years of hunting in Central Africa. But in the end, Gert got the better of me. In camp I had what I considered was the finest and largest leopard skin I had ever seen. I had gone to a lot of trouble to cure and soften the skin, and Gert immediately fastened on to it. For days he kept pestering me to sell the skin to him, and I finally agreed to let him have it in exchange for a pair of powerful binoculars which he promised to send me immediately on his return to South Africa. This was ten years ago, and I am still waiting for that pair of binoculars. The chances of my ever receiving them are, however, extremely remote as Gert came to grief when he was killed by a rhino in Kenya a couple of years after our memorable hunt in the Usanga Plains.

If Gert figured at the one end of the scale, a young German I met in Tanganyika some years earlier certainly filled the role at the other end. At that time I had not been able to hunt for fully a year, owing to a bad spell of sun-glare which caused me to see double. It was a week before Easter, and I had a friend from Rhodesia visiting me. He was particularly anxious to join in a hunting safari and as I could not fill the shooting role, I appealed to my old friend, Charlie Goss, the elephant hunter, to organize a safari for Easter week-end.

Charlie promptly took the matter in hand and made all the necessary arrangements for a good outing. The transportation of the safari was entrusted to a German, Franz, who was running a transport business in the vicinity.

That week-end we spent four days in the bush and walked scores of miles. At the end of that time we had accounted for only one reed-buck. It was a disastrous trip, but typical of hunters' luck.

When Franz called for his cheque the day after our return, I was very voluble in expressing my disappointment at the result of the trip. After I had finished bemoaning our bad luck, he assured me that he knew of a place 75 miles away where game was exceedingly plentiful. He was prepared to take us out on another trip that week-end on a ' no results, no pay ' basis. He undertook to attend to all the details of the safari, including food and drinks, and I would settle with him on our return.

Early that Saturday morning we set out for the Usanga Plains. Charlie Goss again accompanied us and, for good measure, he brought along another well-known big-game hunter. Although I did not intend to do any hunting, I took my light sporting Westly Richards .318 rifle. When camp was eventually installed that afternoon there was something of the bizarre about it. Franz had brought every conceivable kind of canned food and drinks. He had made up his mind to do things in style, and it was quite obvious that he was no amateur at the game. For an ordinary truck-driver he certainly set me wondering.

Later that afternoon we drove out for our first shoot, and it was not long before we spotted the first game—a small herd of impala. The animals were extremely timid, and in the end the two marksmen were obliged to open up at 300 yards range. In quick time they both emptied their magazines on the running antelopes—ten shots, without a single hit. By now the range had widened to close on 500 yards. It was at that moment that Franz asked me if I would allow him a shot or two with my rifle. As he lifted the rifle it was immediately obvious that he was no greenhorn at the game. In spite of the extreme range, Franz took two quick shots; I could not see what the result was, but as he handed back the rifle to me he remarked, ' I managed to get two, but they are too far away now for more shooting '. Franz was quite right.

As we followed the trail of the herd, we came on two impalas lying a few yards apart. Up to this time Franz had never mentioned that he had done any worth-while hunting before, but his astonishing marksmanship intrigued me so much that I immediately started questioning him.   It was only then that I learned that he had hunted on the Serengeti Plains for several years and that he had taken out numerous big hunting parties, including an Indian maharajah.   After this incident I frequently watched Franz performing.   His shooting was something fantastic.   On one occasion I watched him run at full speed for more than 100 yards, come to a sudden stop, and bring down a running buck 300 yards away.   This extraordinary performance was easier to understand when I found out later that he was a freak, with a pulse of forty.

Throughout the three days we remained on the plain Franz gave daily demonstrations of the most amazing marksmanship. Had he claimed at the time that he was the finest game-shot in all Africa I would have supported his claim.   I never got to know what his complete hunting record was; getting anything out of Franz was like sucking blood from a stone.   With one tenth the bombast of Gert, he would have held any audience spell-bound.

But Franz was a lethargic, casual type of person who could not spare the time or energy for wild talk.   Nothing ever took him out of his stride.   A charging or a running buffalo looked exactly the same to him.   In subsequent years I got to know him very well and shared many safaris with him.   On the trail he could carry on for days with a flask of water and little or no food.   He was frequently in trouble with the Game Department, but always had the right answers, and never more so than on the occasion when he shot a sable antelope for which he had no licence.   The hooves were carefully collected by a police officer, and were then put into a bag and placed in the officer's car.   After this was done Franz invited the officer to have a cup of tea.   The house-boy was a Kavironda whose language no one but Franz could speak.   Ostensibly giving the native instructions to prepare the tea, Franz actually instructed him to replace the sable hooves with those of an ox he had killed that morning.   After tea the officer departed with the necessary evidence for the prosecution of the case.   I was not present when the bag was opened, and have often wondered just how that officer felt when he discovered the trick Franz had played on him; when he returned to Franz's camp the next day all the evidence had disappeared, and the case had to be dropped.

When war broke out Franz was one of the first to be rounded up. In view of his reputation as a deadly shot, the troopers who were sent to bring him in fully expected to figure in a shooting match with him, but Franz gave no trouble on that occasion. It was later, on his way to South Africa for internment, that he presented his guards with serious trouble, for somewhere between Dar-es-Salaam and Pretoria, Franz mysteriously disappeared. He has never been heard of since, but I have a vague suspicion that he has settled down comfortably somewhere in South Africa.

CHAPTER XVI

GREAT HUNTERS OF THE PAST

DURING THE LATTER end of 1944 I was engaged on 'priority' war work, and part of my job consisted in supplying foodstuffs of every description for a labour gang of some 2,000 Africans. This called for a great deal of hunting, as meat could be obtained only from game. Cattle or any other domestic animals, for that matter, could not be raised in the area owing to the prevalence of tsetse. I had an open permit to shoot any animal worth shooting for its meat—elephant, rhino, and giraffe only excepted.

The district, however, compensated to some extent for its shortage of meat by large supplies of maize which the local inhabitants cultivated. One of the most fertile maize-producing areas was badly handicapped by transportation difficulties, the primary cause of which was the Kafufu River, which flowed all the year round, making crossing with lorries extremely difficult. To overcome this difficulty it was decided to construct a suitable bridge at the most advantageous point, and soon some 200 natives were actively employed on the project. For a time all went well, and the work was nearing completion when the headman arrived one morning to report that a rogue elephant had completely disorganized the work the day before. A large number of the wooden pillars had been uprooted, and most of the labourers had fled from the scene, and refused to return to work.

It would have been a simple matter for me to have gone out and destroyed this troublesome animal, but my licence did not permit me to shoot elephant. It is true the game laws in Tanganyika Territory permit one to destroy any animal that causes damage to property, but there is a catch in the regulation, which provides that such an animal must be 'caught in the act'. I went out on two consecutive days—a distance of 75 miles—but failed to catch the rogue 'in the act'. Meanwhile a report had been sent to the game warden of the district and permission asked for me to deal with the elephant. Before we received a reply to this communication the bull paid a second visit to the bridge, and this time he completed his work of destruction to such an extent that hardly a pillar was left standing erect. The remnants of the labour force had fled, and for all I know some of them may still be running.

It was a day after this second outrage that we received a reply to our communication to the Game Department. The department was not prepared to grant permission for unauthorized persons to destroy elephants indiscriminately; a member of the warden's staff would come out to investigate the position and see that the elephant was driven away or, if necessary, destroyed.

A few days later the warden's representative, a young man in his early twenties, accompanied by three native game scouts, arrived at our camp in a vanette well stocked with rifles, ammunition, and camp equipment. That evening the young man spent in my camp, and for some time we talked hunting and hunters, until finally the conversation came to the subject uppermost in both our minds—the rogue bull of the Kafufu River. I was surprised to gather from my guest that, whereas he had previously sent in hundreds of reports on game movements during his three years' service, and had also done a fair amount of control shooting, he had never had to deal with a rogue elephant. This was to be his first attempt in this direction—a tough assignment indeed.

At one stage of our conversation that night I was almost tempted to offer my assistance to the young man; it was obvious that he was nervous and not at all in love with the job. The thought of the off-handed manner in which the department had treated the application for me to attend to the trouble, however, decided me against having any more to do with the elephant—a decision I have since deeply regretted, for it was only two days later that one of the game scouts came in to report that his master had been killed by the rogue bull after it had been severely wounded. The bull then departed from the area, and before a further month had elapsed he accounted for yet another game scout. His reign of terror came to an end one morning when a mining engineer from an adjoining property 100 miles away put paid to his account after he himself had narrowly escaped being killed by the bull.

This was in *1944*. In 1934 I applied for a licence to shoot two elephants. The licence was duly granted after I had parted company with £50. On issuing the licence, however, the official took care to draw my attention to the fact that I was allowed to *hunt* two elephants. There is a subtle difference between *hunting* and *killing*. For instance, if I were to follow an elephant for a given distance and lost trace of him, I would have hunted him. If I succeeded in wounding an elephant and failed to collect him, I would also have *hunted* him and there would be one elephant less on my licence. At £25 per peep, this kind of elephant *hunting* can be very costly—more so when the country is full of informers who share in the proceeds of any fine imposed as the result of their information.

The reason why I have turned the clock back twenty-two years to record these two cases is that I have been wondering for some time when the era of great hunters in Africa really came to an end. It is quite a common thing these days to pick up a book or a newspaper review in which it is claimed that some author or other is ' the last of the great African hunters ', ' the finest shot that ever lived ', and many other attributes which, in the nature of things, are completely out of place. Present-day restrictions, control by the various game departments, the setting aside of huge tracts of country as game reserves and sanctuaries, have long since cramped the style of the modern hunter to such an extent that there is mighty little he can do to qualify for a title of greatness when compared with the generation that passed by some thirty or more years ago.

It is of interest to review some of the really great hunters of the past so that the reader of today may judge for himself. A close personal association with many of the famous old-timers and my own record of over thirty years in the hunting field should be of some assistance to me in assessing the merits of the great figures who have passed over the African hunting scene.

No hunting history of Africa could be written without the inclusion of the great Selous. Like Paganini of violin fame, Selous always overshadows every other figure in the hunting game. But as in the case of Paganini, there are few standards by which accurate comparisons can be made, and just as, rightly or wrongly, Kubelik once claimed that the very technique which made Paganini a celebrity in his day is today the stock-in-trade of every successful violinist, so also it may be claimed with equal justification that the methods and technique employed by the famous Selous is the stock-in-trade of almost every serious hunter in the African field today. I pause to allow time for the worshippers at the shrine of Selous to pass judgment on me for this perfidy.

But it so happens that I was once privileged to accompany Selous on a two months' safari in the Shangani district of Southern Rhodesia. He was then gathering material for his book *Sunshine and Storm in Rhodesia*. My step-father at that time was the proprietor of a successful transport organization, the motive power of which was my old friend the donkey. I was a boy of about twelve, and as this trip was organized during the school holidays, I was able to join the expedition. Among the drivers employed in our organization was one van der Westhuizen. Van had recently returned from what was then German South-West Africa, where he was employed by the Germans as a scout in the Herero rebellion.

At that time the name of Selous was a household word all over Rhodesia and both v.d. Westhuizen and I were over-awed by the reputation of the great hunter. Night after night we sat round the camp-fires and listened in wonder to the stories he told, but soon the time came for Selous to give us a practical demonstration of his prowess. I would go on record by saying that one of the most amazing exhibitions of indifferent marksmanship I ever saw in the field was provided by the famous Selous.

The debunking started on an open plain one morning when the target was a reedbuck, and the range roughly 200 yards. On this occasion I saw Selous empty two magazines (ten shots) at a standing and moving target which never exceeded 400 yards, and failed to register one single hit. It was only after Selous had emptied his second magazine that v.d. Westhuizen went into action. By this time the range exceeded 400 yards. Like Selous, v.d. Westhuizen was using a 9.3-mm. rifle. The shot was taken from a standing position without a gun-rest and was put fairly and squarely in the heart. It is true that v.d. Westhuizen never gained fame as a hunter, but in German West Africa he had the reputation of being the finest shot among the troops then operating against the Hereros.

During the course of the next two months I witnessed many similar exhibitions of marksmanship between the two men. As a shot, Selous was never in the same class—a fact he freely admitted. Selous attributed his poor marksmanship to paralysed shoulder-muscles—a relic of the price he paid in his early career when he was forced to use the old blunderbusses of that time—often with an excessive charge of powder and the resulting damage to the shooter.

It was, however, only in the matter of marksmanship that Selous figured in this unfavourable light. As a hunter he had forgotten more than v.d. Westhuizen ever learned. Selous had the knowledge of animals and their habits, especially when the chips were down, that always remained a closed book to v.d. Westhuizen.

The point was well demonstrated one afternoon when Van got on the wrong side of a wounded buffalo. Always the deadly perfect shot, he overstepped the mark just once too often, and stood waiting for a charging ' buff ' until only a few yards separated them. When he squeezed the trigger, there was no response. He could hardly have realized that he had drawn a misfire before the enraged bull was on top of him, and he did not live long enough to learn where he had gone wrong. It is extremely unlikely that such an accident could ever have happened to Selous, the perfect hunter, but indifferent shot.

During the two months of this safari I was thrilled daily by the marvellous exhibition of marksmanship on the part of v.d. Westhuizen, and at that time I would have emulated the example of present-day scribes and declared v.d. Westhuizen the greatest ever hunter. In the light of subsequent events I am not quite so sure now. Most of the great hunters I have known have died in their beds. The others were not so lucky. Selous was undoubtedly a great hunter, but an even greater naturalist. It must not be forgotten that in his day there were no restrictions of any kind. Game reserves did not exist in the areas where he hunted. Game was plentiful everywhere, and some of the districts in which he did his best hunting are today thickly populated, without a vestige of wild life.

It was many years later that Selous and I were again operating in the same area, but this time big game was not the quarry. We were serving as scouts for the British Forces in German East Africa. Selous was then a man well in his sixties, and had no business to be in that part of the world on such a dangerous mission. I was sitting in camp in Abercorn, Northern Rhodesia, one night when the news came through that he had been killed in action earlier that day. Given the choice, this is probably the way he would have chosen to make his exit. R.I.P.

Then there was the great W. D. M. Bell. I write of him in the past only in so far as his hunting is concerned. A few years ago he was still hale and hearty, and busy on yet another book on his hunting days. In the Kavironda country, where he was best known, it will be a daring man who would attempt to rate him second to any other hunter—past or present. The present-day elephant hunter takes the greatest care to see that he is suitably equipped with the most modern and heaviest express rifles when any of the big ' beef trusts ' happen to be the quarry. Let us turn the spotlight on Kavironda Bell, as he is affectionately known.

Bell rarely if ever used anything heavier than an 8 mm., and a great many elephants were accounted for with a toy 7 mm. It is not necessary to explain that for a hunter to tackle elephants with that kind of weapon he had to be a dead crack shot and be certain of a kill each time he squeezed a trigger. Bell undoubtedly had many narrow escapes in dealing with such massive animals with such light guns, but of all the ' greatest hunters ' and the ' greatest shots ' of today, is there one who will persistently take the field against elephant, rhino, buffalo, lion, etc., with a rifle that is generally used only to ' provide for the pot ' ? Bell's marksmanship has become legendary throughout Uganda and in many other Central African territories. Not only was he one of the finest shots in the history of African hunting, he was also a master craftsman at the game. The proof? When last I heard of him he was well over eighty years of age. It was not only good shooting, but first-class hunting that kept him on deck all those years, and do not forget, his score for elephants runs well into four figures—all accounted for with the lightest of sporting rifles.

The spotlight now moves on to my old friend, Micky Norton, the father and, if you wish, the grandfather of all elephant hunters, with a score of over 4,000 elephants to his credit—collected during sixty active years in the field. I had the pleasure and honour to accompany Micky on many occasions and I have often seen him in action. Micky was instrumental in perfecting the modern .318 Westley Richards rifle, and he rarely used a heavier calibre against elephant. Even after he quarrelled with the Westley concern he fell back on a light 8-mm. rifle. An Irishman, standing fully 6 feet 4 inches and weighing over sixteen stone, he was always my ideal of the perfect hunter and bushman. There was nothing in the technique of elephant hunting that Micky did not know by heart; and was there ever a man to surpass him in courage? In his prime I would rate him as one of the most deadly shots I ever saw, and this, combined with his knowledge and experience, places him high on my list of great African hunters.

I was privileged to join Micky on several of his notable safaris and watched him perform in all kinds of circumstances. There was the time in the Belgian Congo when ivory was worth twenty-two shillings per lb. Elephants were plentiful, but the Belgian authorities in those days could not appreciate the urgency of an application for a licence to hunt them. Frequently six months or more would lapse before an application would be attended to. During those six months we hunters fell back on our natural resources—poaching—shoot first, and explain afterwards—if necessary.

It was whilst Micky and I were down in the Back Congo—living on our resources—that he survived one of the most amazing elephant adventures ever to befall any hunter. As usual, we started out in opposite directions one morning. There was plenty of evidence of elephants in the vicinity. Micky chose the north side of the river, whilst I took the south. Late that afternoon I returned with two prize trophies to my credit, but there was no sign of Micky. All that night I sat up awaiting his return, but when at daybreak next day he had still not arrived, I felt that the worst had happened to him.

After a hurried breakfast I got the spotters and trackers on the way to trace his trail of the previous day. Late that afternoon we came to the steep banks of a tributary of the Congo River. Deep down the ravine we could hear Micky calling for help. At that moment he lay buried under hundreds of branches and tree-trunks, and he was lucky indeed to be alive.

Earlier the previous day he had dropped a prize bull, and it was whilst he sat admiring the tusks of his trophy that he suddenly found himself at the end of a charge from the infuriated herd. Instinctively he ran for the river and slid down its steep banks. The descent was too steep for the herd to negotiate, but that did not deter them from having a try at settling the score. The next instant Micky found himself being covered under an avalanche of branches and young trees which the herd were tossing down on him. They were making a determined effort to bury him alive, and this assault lasted until darkness set in, when the herd must have decided that he was effectively taken care of and moved away. It took us more than an hour to extricate Micky from his unenviable position. No one but Micky Norton could have survived that leafy fusillade. This is only one of many hair-raising adventures I shared with my old friend.

I was not with him some years previously, during his hectic career in German East Africa, before the First World War. Here Micky ran amok for some time, and shot up elephants at such a rate that the authorities finally decided to take action—an unheard-of thing in those days. For days an officer with a batch of askaris stuck to Micky's trail down the Ruhaha River. Finally, when the going got too rough, Micky occupied a small island in the river. Here he ran up the Union Jack and proclaimed that spot British territory. From this stronghold he made it known that he was prepared to shoot it out with anybody who disagreed with him on that point. It was only as the result of intervention by the Colonial Office that Micky finally decided to vacate this piece of ' British territory ' in German East Africa.

It may not be generally known that possibly the finest book ever written on elephant hunting, compiled for Micky by a ' ghost writer ', is lying with a London publisher, where it has been for more than twenty-five years. Micky quarrelled, first with his ' ghost ', then with the prospective publisher.   In the end he refused to allow the book to be published.   This was the position when he died in 1946.   At that time I had made good progress with him with a view to having the manuscript released for publication.   When I left him for my last elephant hunt that night he promised me faithfully that he would come to an arrangement with me on my return.   But that was to be the last I ever saw of my old friend.   When I arrived back at my main camp three weeks later he had already been buried eight days.   For courage, nerve, bushcraft, and marksmanship, no hunter has ever surpassed Micky Norton.   He was one of Africa's all-time greats.

Let us take a glimpse at the record of Tim Downing of Back Congo and Baluba Country fame.   It was Tim who guided the naval expedition from Simonstown to Lake Tanganyika—one of the most amazing exploits of the First World War.   It was this expedition that put paid to the account of the German gunboat which was then operating on Lake Tanganyika, and had for years proved a thorn in the side of British military leaders in East Africa.   Tim was brought all the way down from the Belgian Congo to take the expedition across country on to Lake Tanganyika, and he was probably the only man in Africa capable of leading such an expedition over the hazardous route they had to follow.

Tim started life as a bank clerk and ended his career as chief accountant in that institution.   It was then that he decided to try the hunting business—an unfortunate love affair having prompted him to take to the bush.   Early in his hunting career he teamed up with Joe Dubbin, who all but succeeded in overthrowing the Belgian Colonial Government of that time and establishing a republic, which he intended to name after himself.   I have related the details of this affair in my previous book—*Horned Death*.

Like myself, Tim found excitement and adventure on the trail of the buffalo.   For many years he was occupied on control work for the Belgian Government in the Congo, and not even Tim himself can tell how many buffaloes he accounted for during twenty years on that trail.   Certain it is that he holds the all-time high record for an individual effort—and that was twenty-one buffaloes in twenty-one shots.   This happened during an organized hunt on the bend of the Congo River, where buffalo was declared vermin by reason of the spread of tsetse, which killed thousands of natives in one of the worst epidemics of sleeping sickness ever known in Central Africa. Apart from buffaloes, Tim's elephant score also ran into four figures. When finally he decided to call it a day he had only one regret, and that was that after thirty years in the field he had never once succeeded in bagging a lion.

It was not many years later that I again caught up with Tim. We had both migrated to Tanganyika Territory, where we eventually joined the staff of a lead-mining company during the latter part of the last war. I often called on Tim, who was camped only a few miles from me. On these occasions we always reminisced about the old Congo hunting days, but Tim always bemoaned his bad luck in so far as lion was concerned. Then, one morning, a gang of wood-cutters came in to report to me that they were being menaced by a lion which they thought showed man-eating tendencies.

I immediately sent a message to Tim and suggested to him that he took advantage of this opportunity of bagging a lion. Tim, however, was not impressed by the natives' story and did not think it worth while to walk 8 miles on a wild-goose chase. Next day the natives again came in to appeal for help. It was quite obvious that they were terrified, and I decided to go after the troublesome lion. At twelve o'clock that night I lined up a 10-foot specimen in the sights of a .333 Jeffery and subsequently loaded him up in a covered vanette.

Early next morning I sent requesting Tim to call at my camp, and on his arrival I asked him to open the back flap of the vanette. Staring him in the face were the wide-open jaws of the lion I had accounted for the previous evening. That was the last straw! The idea of missing what was probably his last opportunity of ever getting a lion proved too much for Tim, and the next instant he burst into a flood of tears whilst, with his one hand, he sat gently stroking the head of the dead lion. This lion certainly deserved sympathy and tears at the time of our encounter. Like so many of his type, he had previously fallen foul of a porcupine; in the ensuing struggle several quills had become embedded in his paws and jaws, where they had set up festering sores. As a result he was unable to hunt down his prey, and at the time of our meeting he was thoroughly emaciated and on the point of turning man-eater.

On the buffalo—as also on the elephant trail—Tim was a deadly shot, and a first-class hunter. The proof? He survived forty years of intensive hunting and lives to tell the story. Like the rest of the great hunters, his active career came to an end some twenty-five years ago, but up to the end he remained a sentimentalist. On the morning after a narrow escape with a buffalo he decided it was time to ' pack up ', and went down to the Congo River and tossed his favourite .404 into its flowing waters. Tim did not think any other man was good enough to use that gun, and he refused to accept my cash offer for it.

The spotlight turns to Major Pretorius—' the Wizard of the Bush '. His own book, *Jungle Man*, gives such a complete account of his activities in the hunting-field that there is no need for me to enlarge upon it. Pretorius and I had a great deal in common, inasmuch as we covered almost identical territories—German East Africa, Congo, Back Congo, Ituri, etc. For years he was a thorn in the side of the German Government, and they set hundreds of traps for him without success. In the end they decided to confiscate his farm and other property. Pretorius retaliated by shooting a dozen prize elephant bulls and disposing of the ivory to advantage, and finally levelled the score by leading the British expedition which sank the German gunboat in the backwaters of Dar-es-Salaam during the last war.

His epic walk of over 100 miles through the Kalahari Desert in order to settle the score with a leopard which had previously mauled his brother, is an indication of his determination. The tricky job he completed for the South African Government in shooting elephant in the Addo Bush was a masterpiece of craftsmanship. If anyone were to take the initiative and declare him the greatest hunter of them all, I should have little to quarrel about. I quarrel, however, with one claim made on his behalf, and that is that he succeeded in dropping five charging elephants in five shots, in a time record of thirty-five seconds—and that with a .365 medium rifle. That kind of shooting is completely ' out of this world ' and too much even for a Pretorius.

There were, indeed, many other famous 'old-timers', and a complete account of their activities would fill several volumes and might, in the end, become tiresome. Barnes, Bishop, Sutherland, Goss, Bacon, Cooper, van Rooyen, Grobler. The latter, at sixty-five years of age, once found himself in the unenviable position of seeing a wounded lion drag his only son through close bush. The range was 200 yards, and conditions permitted very little time for careful aim. It was split-second shooting that dropped the lion in its tracks without touching the son, who escaped from the ordeal with only superficial wounds. That I consider marksmanship of a very high order indeed.

Charlie Goss, who always preferred the double .600 Jeffery, until one afternoon when he had to look for safety in the tree-tops after a spot of bother with an elephant. Seated high up on a massive branch, he applied the final touch by pulling both triggers simultaneously; the recoil knocked him clean off his perch and landed him on top of the dying elephant.

Charlie also had over a thousand elephants to his credit and was a deadly shot—a fact he often demonstrated to the habitues of the bars in Dar-es-Salaam. On these occasions he would stage a William Tell act for their benefit. The guinea-pig for these exhibitions was an old gun-bearer—an empty beer-bottle replacing the apple. The act remained very popular until one night Charlie missed the bottle and placed a .22 slug in the ear of his accomplice. A £20 fine helped to cure Charlie of this eccentricity. Charlie 'did' the Ubangi, the Kivu, Ituri Forest, Kenya, Tanganyika, and many other tight haunts, and any hunter who could survive that kind of business for forty years is no mean hunter. His hunting days came to a close when he became completely paralysed in Tanganyika some twenty years ago.

Who was the greatest of them all?

Your guess is as good as mine.

One thing is certain, there have been no real GREAT HUNTERS during the past twenty-five years. The existing conditions— game control, which limits a hunter to only a few head of game on a licence, the numerous sanctuaries, and many other re- strictions, have cramped the style of the present-day hunter,

L

and have done so for many years. It is all for the good, and it is better to have thousands of heads of game of every kind walking about unmolested—so long as they molest no one— than to have hundreds of hunters with thousands of carcasses to their credit.

CHAPTER XVII

WHEN THE UNEXPECTED HAPPENS

'It is always easy to be wise *after* an event', is an old saying that can be applied in the hunting business more often than in any other. How often, in discussing a hunting casualty, have I not heard it said that if the victim had not done this, that, or the other, he would still be alive.

It should be quite obvious to any thinking person that in a business where fatal accidents may occur at any moment, no serious hunter deliberately does something foolish that is likely to result in his name figuring in the obituary column. One might as well say, in speaking of the dead in everyday normal life, that if he had not stopped breathing he would still be alive. There is no doubt that many of the hunting accidents in Africa are due to carelessness and miscalculations, but in a game where the unexpected and the unforeseen so often happen, one cannot always take all the precautions necessary to safeguard one against each and every contingency.

Looking over the score-card carefully, I am convinced that on at least a dozen occasions I also qualified for the 'he should not have . . .' category. The fact that I did not meet with an untimely end, I attribute to a generous slice of luck. It is difficult to explain why the best and most experienced hunters sometimes take chances which may, and do, end in tragedy. But a good many accidents happen because the best calculations go all wrong, and when they do, one is not left with sufficient time to rectify the position.

You wound an elephant, buffalo, or lion, and he disappears in tall grass or close shrub. You follow the blood trail, and are convinced that it is a heart or lung shot from which the animal *must* die in a very short time. The country is too treacherous to take chances, and you go back to camp feeling quite certain that by next morning the animal will be dead. Next day you return; for a moment you have lost your bearings, and you are looking for the exact spot where you left the trail the day before. It is whilst you are still looking for the trail that there is a sudden charge from close quarters. The animal did *not* die overnight, and may even have walked back on its tracks to where the shooting took place in the first instance. You have walked into such a hornet's nest, and you qualify for a post-mortem by others who know better.

There were at least three occasions on which I escaped by the proverbial skin of my teeth, when I did not take wilful risks, nor could the resulting trouble be attributed to miscalculations in so far as actual hunting is concerned, and it was luck alone that saved me from a post-mortem. On the Southern Highlands of Tanganyika I once took out a party of four Italians on an elephant hunt. They were well equipped with the latest heavy-calibre sporting rifles and, in addition, they had brought out an old-type cine camera with which to record the most exciting incidents of the trip.

Shortly after two o'clock one afternoon we came across an old tusker standing fast asleep under a big tree, quite near to dense forest. The target was so easy, and the range so close, that I did not for a moment doubt that my companions would easily account for the bull. It was decided that I would raise and drop my hat three times; on the fall of the hat for the third time they would all four shoot simultaneously. Throughout the trip so far I had acted as camera-man, and here also I would play the dual role of photographer and signaller.

On the fall of the hat for the third time all four shots rang out. The bull, instead of dropping to the fusillade, made a wild swerve, and immediately disappeared in the thick forest. We followed the blood trail for a short distance, and it was apparent that at least one shot had pierced a lung. In the case of elephant, buffalo, rhino, and such-like big animals, unless both lungs are pierced they will live for many hours before finally giving up the ghost, and it is when they are so seriously and mortally wounded that their tempers become badly ruffled. In the present case the bush was so dense, and the marksmanship of my companions so indifferent, that I decided not to follow the trail too far.

A few hundred yards from where the shooting had taken place was a large water-pool where elephants regularly came to drink; around it was fairly open country. I felt convinced that if this bull had taken a slug in one of his lungs and could survive the injury for any length of time, he would inevitably make for water. I suggested therefore that we mount a high bank at the near end of the pool, place the camera in position, and wait for the bull to come to drink.

My suggestion that I should take one of the side positions of the pool to make sure of the shooting was not acceptable to my companions; they all wanted to figure in the picture showing them bringing down a prize trophy. In the end I reluctantly accepted the proposition.

It was arranged that two of them would take up their positions on either side of the pool, and hide behind the bushes skirting it. I would occupy the central position on the high bank, from where I could take in the entire show. The bull was expected to approach the water on a well-worn elephant path. Shooting was to begin as soon as he started drinking, by which time the marksman would have closed in sufficiently to figure in the picture I would take. The stalking of the bull whilst at water, the final disposal of the elephant—all would be realistically portrayed in this masterpiece of filming.

It was fully an hour before we heard the bull coming through the dense forest. From the manner in which we could hear trees being pushed down I concluded that he was in a bad way —this was a minor miscalculation. Everything was in order now, and I was at my post with a black cloth over my head, ready to start operations as soon as the bull came into view. A few yards to my left was my heavy-calibre rifle, resting against a tree.

The bull, however, did not approach the pool from the expected quarter. He had, in fact, passed uncomfortably close to where the two Italians on his right had taken cover behind some dense scrub. Now he was walking towards the water at a fast pace, whilst I kept turning the handle of the camera, which I had hidden as best I could behind the meagre cover. At any minute now the bull would be at the edge of the water and the final scene of this epic picture enacted. It was at that moment that he must have seen or scented me, for he gave forth a shrill cry and stretched his ears out wide, raising his trunk high above his head. He was still a good

50 yards off, and I was working away at top speed, expecting to hear four shots being fired at any moment.

But there were no shots, and by the time I could get out from under the black cloth the bull was already coming towards me in full charge. I escaped that charge by a matter of yards, and it was just as the bull was busy hurling the camera to the ground that I managed to line him up in my sights and place a brain-shot which brought the proceedings to an end. Of my four companions there was not a sign to be seen in the vicinity.

It was several minutes after proceedings had come to an end, and in response to my calling, that the first of them showed up behind a tree some distance away. A few minutes later the other three appeared sheepishly on the scene—minus their rifles, which they had discarded in their undignified flight—a man cannot run fast nor can he climb a tree with a rifle in his hands.

From their subsequent explanations I gathered that things went all wrong from the moment the elephant had failed to follow the programme I had visualized. When he failed to appear on the path which I had expected him to follow, they were at a loss how to act. When he spread his ears and gave forth that blood-curdling cry, they were at no loss what to do, and they decided there and then to put as much distance between them and the elephant as possible and in the quickest possible time, fully expecting me to do likewise, or extricate myself out of the difficulty as best I could. I decided that this was as good a point as any for the safari to start on its way back home. I had almost lost my life that afternoon, but my friends lost all there was of their camera and whatever prospects there may have been of a film depicting them in the forefront of African hunters.

The next time I was nearly led into a death-trap was when I took Congo with me to help follow the trail in difficult country. Congo was the quaint offspring of a dachshund mother and a bull mastiff father. He was one of a litter of seven, and the only one to inherit the best traits of his parents—intelligence and tenacity. I had often used him with complete success to trail wounded buck in tall grass. On these occasions he proved absolutely fearless, and lost no time in getting to grips with wounded animals. The largest of antelopes inspired no fear in him, and once he had fastened his fangs in either throat or nose of a wounded buck, he would hold on grimly until I arrived on the scene and took over.

Up to the time of which I now write I had never had an opportunity to test Congo against a wounded buffalo. I had no doubt though that should a wounded buffalo enter difficult country, Congo would help to find him and keep him at bay until I could do the necessary. That morning Congo was taken out on a leash, and we were soon on the trail of a herd. By 10 a.m. I had lined up a magnificent bull in my sights. The resulting shot was well placed in the chest, but the bull took off at high speed and entered tall grass before I could venture another shot.

There was a heavy blood trail, and I firmly believed that I had placed a heart shot, or that both lungs had been pierced, owing to the short range and the high-powered rifle I was using. I had no doubt the bull would not survive for many minutes, and I decided to wait for a few moments in an open patch before releasing Congo to go on the trail. If the bull was still alive, Congo would keep him at bay until I could come up. If not, he would bark for a bit, and if I did not follow him immediately, he would come back to call me.

It was barely a minute after Congo had disappeared on the trail when I heard a vicious snort, and this was followed immediately by loud yelping. The next instance Congo came rushing towards me at full speed; close on his heels was the infuriated bull, snorting and billowing froth from his nostrils. It was lucky for me that I had selected an open clearing which gave me an uninterrupted view of fully 50 yards, and the yelping had put me on guard. When that bull took a dive as the result of a well-placed bullet between its eyes, the distance separating us was no more than 10 yards. This was another sound calculation that went on the rocks.

Congo was thoroughly disgraced, and even after the bull was killed he would not approach it, but kept walking round it in wide circles, all the time baring his fangs at the dead animal. He certainly had no heart for buffalo troubles, and after that I never again took him on the trail when buffalo was the quarry. But Congo was not unique in the matter of buffalo-baiting. Dogs that will give excellent results on the large antelopes will definitely shy off when it comes to buffalo. The reason is that a badly wounded antelope will rarely put up a determined charge if approached too closely by a dog. Generally they will snort loudly and swing their heads from side to side. A charge, if molested in such circumstances, is never sustained and the dog is never really seriously menaced.

With the buffalo it is different. When he is on the defensive and approached within charging distance, there is no side play: the bosses go down, there is a vicious snort, froth billows forth from both nostrils, and there is a menacing bellowing throughout the charge. It wants a very brave and determined adversary to face this bundle of unbridled fury once the chips are down. The largest and best-trained hunting dogs have sense enough to know and follow the wisdom of the old adage that discretion is the better part of valour.

By contrast, an old friend of mine who has had more practical experience of hunting dogs, assures me that the little fox terriers are in no way put out by an angry buffalo. He quoted many instances when he had sat and watched a group of them play a buffalo out until he was so utterly fatigued that he abandoned all active aggressive tendencies. He quoted several instances when he had watched one of these diminutive little warriors fasten on to a buffalo's nose and hang on grimly until the end. I have no reason to disbelieve my friend, but after the experience with Congo I always felt happier and safer to fall back on my own resources when the trail got difficult. Who knows, this may be the reason why I have not been subjected to a post-mortem by hunters who do not believe in dogs when the going gets tough!

Another occasion when my own calculations were not at fault, yet I narrowly escaped serious trouble with a male lion, was when a friend and I were hunting on the Usanga Plains in Tanganyika Territory. It was after the brute had made two raids on our meat-piles.[1]

I decided it was time to curb his activities, and that night a

[1] In these days, when a day's salary buys barely sufficient meat for a good meal, it is as well to explain what is meant by a meat-pile. At the end of a day's hunting it is often all but impossible to get the meat into camp, where it has to be dissected and smoked next day. When one hunts to keep as many as 2000 natives provided with meat, the enterprise assumes major proportions.

big bait was put out for him. The only drawback was that we could not place the bait near a tree from where we could attend to the raider. The plain was barren so far as trees were concerned, and in order to create a suitable cover for ourselves, we had slung up a rough grass cover, mounted on sticks. The grass was packed very close to the ground and offered a reasonably good camouflage at night. George, my friend, although a good hunter, had had no previous experience with lions, but he was anxious to take part in the night's adventure.

For the occasion we took with us our two heavy-calibre sporting rifles, and also a double-barrel shotgun, as additional security in case of trouble. At close quarters a shotgun is as effective a weapon against a charging lion as I can think of. Loaded with the right ammunition, it is infallible, providing the shooter keeps his range within 10 yards or less. Any distance beyond this range is unsafe, as in a charge the mane is usually raised, and the force of the pellets broken down before they reach the brain.

George and I had taken up our vigil shortly after 8 p.m., and between us lay the three loaded weapons—all ready for action. I had previously explained to George that I would use the shotgun only in case of absolute necessity. Our shack was fully 30 yards from the bait, and well beyond the range of a shotgun. The bait was securely tied to spikes in the ground. Should the lion try to remove the bait, we would give him a few seconds before switching on our torch-lights, and treat him to a dose of lead from our heavy calibres.

It was now well past two o'clock in the morning, and the lion had failed to put in an appearance. Half an hour later there was a rustle in the grass and this was followed almost immediately by a vicious snarl, as the lion jumped on to the bait. It was at that moment that George switched on his light, and before I could realize what was happening a shot rang out. In his excitement George had grabbed the shotgun instead of his heavy calibre, and at that range he could have done little more than pepper the lion with hot lead. There was yet another vicious snarl, and this was followed by a headlong rush in our direction. Whether this was a deliberate charge or a dash to escape from further injury, I will never know; but, whatever it was, it would have been distinctly unhealthy to find oneself directly in the path of that rushing lion.

Although I had switched on my torch the moment George had fired, I failed to pick up the eyes in its rays. All I could see was a shadow dashing towards us. There was no time for careful aim, and all I could do was to hope for the best as I squeezed the trigger. There was a loud thud as the bullet struck home, and the next instant a 10-foot specimen lay sprawling a yard or two in front of us. That lucky shot, with a soft-nose bullet, had entered below the throat and all but severed the head from the body. George's precipitate action, which was due solely to inexperience, could easily have landed us in serious trouble. He was so petrified with shock when the lion took off in our direction that it never occurred to him to fire the second barrel—the exact reason why a shotgun is such a reliable weapon against soft-skinned animals when trouble starts at close quarters.

CHAPTER XVIII

ADVENTURES STRANGE AND EXCITING

'WHAT WAS YOUR most exciting adventure in the bush?' is a question I have been asked so often that I have begun to wonder myself just which I would consider my most exciting or strange adventure. Thirty years in the bush is a very long time, and during all those years there were so many strange and exciting adventures that it is quite impossible to give pride of place to any particular one. It is not always necessarily the adventure itself, so much as the conditions applying at the time, that leave the most lasting impressions on the mind.

Certainly my narrowest escape from a slow and painful death, and one which recurs to my mind with the greatest persistency, in spite of the many years that have since elapsed, came one afternoon after I had followed the trail of a buffalo bull for more than 15 miles. I was accompanied by Black, my gun-bearer, and Ndege, the master tracker. We had been on the trail since shortly after daybreak, and on at least three occasions I had caught a fleeting glimpse of the bull as he disappeared in close bush. By three o'clock that afternoon we came to an open clearing, high up on a hillside, and from here, I decided, I would give the country a last thorough going over with a pair of powerful binoculars before abandoning the trail.

The moment I came to a stop I was jerked violently by the shoulder, and heard Black shouting ' *Njoka, Bwana* ' (snake, master) !

As I looked down I saw the wide-open jaws of a monster-size puff-adder snap the merest fraction of an inch from my knee; the neck of the brute was actually grazing my trousers as it struck out, and it was thanks to Black's timely intervention that those deadly fangs were not sunk into my leg. In coming to a stop, I had actually placed my foot on the tail of the reptile, and it immediately struck out at me.

It was one of my careless days, and I had come out without any serum in my haversack. I was at least five hours' walk from camp, and if that snake had struck home, I would never have reached camp alive. Here is an incident that may not appear so serious on paper, but every time I think of those wide-open jaws with the deadly fangs missing me by the width of tissue paper, a cold shiver runs down my spine.

The adventure in itself was bad enough, but it also placed a powerful weapon in the hands of Black. For years after this incident—in fact up to the time of his death—Black regularly did things that drove me into a frenzy, but whenever I remonstrated with him and tried to curb his evil ways, he would remind me of the day when he saved my life.

There was another occasion when, for the second time in my life, I was driven up a tree by a wounded buffalo bull who now stood glowering at me from below, blowing froth from both nostrils. The charge had come so suddenly and from such a short distance that I was unable to put in a finishing shot. In the rush to scale the tree I was obliged to discard my rifle, and I managed to escape the head-on rush by a matter of inches.

I had hardly settled on an outstretched branch, before I became aware of the excited twittering of birds higher up in the branches. The sound was all too familiar to me, and I immediately started scanning the branches in search of the snake which, I felt certain, had caused the alarm among the birds. A few seconds later my attention was drawn to a movement higher up in the tree, and to my horror, I saw a long green snake crawling slowly down in my direction.

For a moment I sat petrified with fear; from below I was being menaced by a badly wounded bull, still showing plenty of signs of life and aggressiveness, whilst from above a snake which I believed to be a green mamba was slowly closing in on me. It was a terrifying moment, for, apart from a pocket handkerchief, and an ammunition bag round my shoulders, I had nothing with which to defend myself against the snake.

The only thing I could do was to strip a small branch from the limb on which I was sitting; there was just one chance in a million that I might dislodge the snake from the branch and knock it to the ground. With this object in view I quickly started stripping the leaves from the branch. My chances of defending myself with such a puerile weapon were slim indeed, but it must have been the rapid movement in stripping the leaves that attracted the snake's notice; for it suddenly reared up, glared at me for an intense second or two, and then slowly started crawling to an opposite branch.

In a short while I completely lost sight of it in the dense foliage, and I felt reasonably safe; but those two hours until I heard the three long-drawn-out grunts from the dying buffalo were certainly the longest in my life. That bull had shipped a heavy-calibre bullet in the lungs, and, as they usually do when mortally wounded, he had determined to level the score with me. But for the fact that he was losing blood rapidly he might have kept me in the tree for many more hours, and as only about half an hour of daylight remained, my position there, with a deadly poisonous reptile for company in the dark, would have become extremely precarious.

There was another occasion when I was camped near a river at the foot of a high hill. That morning I had left camp on a bicycle to prospect an area where I hoped to find gold. It was late in the afternoon when I returned to camp. A light sporting rifle which I carried to shoot for the pot was securely tied to the bicycle, and I was riding along comfortably with my mind concentrated on the day's work.

I had now reached a steep gradient going down to the river; my eyes were fixed on the narrow path in front of me. A few yards farther on there was a sharp turning which needed con- centration to negotiate at speed. As I took the turning I looked up at the path ahead; I was horrified to see a lion and lioness lying sprawled across it less than 20 yards in front of me. The shock was so great that I instinctively applied the brakes with full force. The next instant I had shot over the handle- bars and lay sprawling in the dust.

It was a terrifying moment when the lion rose slowly and stood looking at me intently for what I thought was several hours. In actual fact the shock was mutual, and as soon as the brute had recovered from his sudden surprise, he made a wild dash into the long grass, with the female following close on his heels. If those lions had been addicted to the eating of human flesh, my adventures in Central Africa would have come to an end there and then. I have often wondered what would have happened to me if the brakes had failed at the critical moment and I had rushed headlong into those two lions lying in the narrow pathway.

Then there was the night at Lake Katavi, in Tanganyika, when I had stuck to the trail too long and returned much later than I had anticipated. It was a black, moonless night, and for miles round the lake the grass grew more than 10 feet high. There were no visible paths leading back to camp, and we were sorting our way through the dense grass with the aid of a small two-cell torch. In order to keep direction, we hugged the shores of the lake through slush and mud. The going was getting more and more difficult when suddenly there was a terrific snorting out towards our right, and this was followed by a wild stampede for the lake.

A large school of hippos had suddenly become aware of our presence and were making a dash for the water. We were right in the path of this avalanche. As I stood there in the dark, waving my torch frantically, I expected to be trampled to death at any moment. It is quite possible that the torch saved me from being overrun, but just how the natives who were following close on my heels escaped death that night I will never know. After the stampede was over I was covered with mud from head to foot—at least one member of that school had passed me so closely that it had splashed mud all over me.

' If we go in for this kind of business too often we'll all wake up one morning and find ourselves dead,' remarked Black when he recovered the power of speech.

Apart from waking up to find myself dead one morning, I decided that it was far too great a strain on the nerves to go walking along the lake-shores on dark nights, and the performance was not repeated. The stampede actually did not last for more than five minutes, but there was a terrific lot of action packed into those few minutes. Standing there in the dark without being able to see as much as an outline of those massive, fear-crazed animals rushing towards one at top speed, was an experience one has to live through to appreciate fully what it feels like.

Perhaps it is true to say that my most tense and terrifying moments in the bush came one morning when, for the second day, I was on the trail of a wounded buffalo. The day before the bull had run down and tossed one of my porters—inflicting a ghastly wound before he was driven off by rapid rifle-fire. A front leg had been smashed below the knee, and this luckily considerably reduced his speed.   The bull was accompanied by four others, and late the previous evening we had abandoned the trail.

This morning we were back on the trail again, and we soon saw the five bulls disappearing in a patch of grass-covered swamp.   We stood for fully half an hour before they emerged on the far side of the swamp.   The sky was heavily overcast and visibility extremely bad.   I could count only four bulls as they walked out of the long grass, but the two trackers with me were convinced that they had counted all five, a dark object, quite close to where the bulls had come to a stop was, they assured me, the wounded animal lying down.

I was far from convinced that this was actually the case, but with the definite assurance of the trackers, who had better eye-sight than mine, I decided to follow the trail through the long grass.   I had hardly walked 100 yards when I noticed a fresh blood track leading off to the right.   Instantly I realized that the bull had gone into ambush—one of the most deadly dangerous situations to cope with in all buffalo-hunting.

For a second I stood petrified with fear.   At any moment I could expect a charge from behind, or the side, in the long grass.   Under the existing conditions there was not the remotest chance of my getting in a shot before the bull would be on top of me.

From an anthill at the edge of the long grass one of the trackers was shouting at me and pointing to his right.   As I followed the direction of the pointing finger I saw the bull on top of a small rise, but it was at that moment that he spotted me too.   This was followed by a vicious grunt, the head was lowered, and out he came in full charge from a distance of about 70 yards.   The charge had no sooner got under way than he disappeared in th 'ong grass: he was rushing to the spot where he had seen me last.   But there was one thing about it: if I could not see the bull, he could not see me either, the wind was luckily in my favour, and he could not pick up my scent.

It was in this desperate situation that I rushed out at right angles to the charge, keeping my head bent low in the long grass. In little more than a couple of seconds that bull rushed past barely 10 yards away from me. For some distance he carried on the charge, and then stood sniffing the air to try to pick up my scent. Soon he started turning in circles, but in the meanwhile I had got out of the danger zone and mounted the anthill, from where I settled my score with the brute. Yes, thinking it all over, this was my most terrifying experience in the bush.

There was still another night when, after a successful day in the field, the natives were sitting gorging themselves at the fireside. Earlier in the day we had noticed numerous rhino spoors in the vicinity and, knowing that these animals are apt to charge a fire at night, I had on several occasions warned the blacks to keep the fire as low as possible and not to make too much noise; but when a native settles down to the flesh-pot, his mind stops functioning and can concentrate only on the feast in front of him.

It was as the voices reached a crescendo and the fire was burning at its brightest that there was a vicious snort quite close to them, and this was followed immediately by the huge frame of a charging rhinoceros. In a fraction of a second the fireside was abandoned and the blacks scattered in all directions, shouting at the top of their voices. But that bull was interested mainly in the fire, which he attacked with great ferocity.

Sitting high up in the back of my open truck, I had a grand-stand view of the whole performance, and watched the rhino venting his spleen until the fire was practically extinguished. Two vicious grunts, undoubtedly to express his satisfaction at his handiwork, terminated the excitement for the night, and the bull walked off into the darkness. During the entire per-formance I had kept him in the sights of a heavy-calibre rifle, expecting as I did that he might pick up my scent and attack the truck, but there was so much fire and smoke flying in all directions that my scent must have evaded him. For the rest of that night I did not hear another sound from the natives, and everything remained in dead silence until shortly after daybreak, when the natives all returned sheepishly to the scene of the night's alarm.

One of the strangest things I ever saw in the bush was when

I dropped a roan bull one afternoon. A gang of Swahili natives were soon on the scene and, after their manner of killing, the throat was slit from side to side. A heavy storm was threatening at the time, and I urged the natives to dissect the carcass as quickly as possible. The head was duly severed and tossed into the waiting truck; after that all the four legs were dissected and loaded. Finally the stomach was opened and all the entrails removed. It was after all this had been done that I noticed the heart still beating inside that small piece of carcass. For several seconds I stood watching that pulsating heart, then, gradually, the movement slowed down, until finally it came to a stop.

I have recorded here what I consider the most exciting—if not the most alarming—experiences I had in the bush. The reader may take his choice as to which one he prefers; but in so doing it is well to remember that he was not on the spot to share my emotions.

M

CHAPTER XIX

THE QUEEN'S GRAVE

'IT ONLY NEEDS a white man who is willing to spend a few pounds and who is not afraid of spirits and witch doctors. If such a man can be found, there will be money for us all. Right now I can do with a new pair of boots, and my clothes are in rags.'

When a native has a proposition to make which entails danger, is downright dishonest, or is risky in the sense that it may bring forth reprisals or supernatural intervention, he will rarely come straight to the point. The method usually is to pick a spot where the person he wishes to interest in an undertaking is likely to overhear a conversation carried on in a loud voice with a friend or accomplice. On this occasion Black was giving free rein to his vocal chords. He had made sure that he would catch me in a place that was isolated and where no one but I and the friend to whom he was talking would overhear the conversation.

Black, at the time, had been with me for more than twenty years. In the bush on our many hunting safaris he was an invaluable servant, fearless and loyal whenever my personal safety and welfare were concerned. On three occasions previously I had saved him from a violent end when he got on the wrong side of wounded buffaloes.

The first time my contribution to his escape was not as remarkable as the manner in which he escaped serious injury—if not death. Black was running towards a tree as fast as his legs could carry him, with an infuriated bull on his trail. I had managed to get in one shot which seriously reduced the bull's speed, but after that I could not shoot again, as Black was in the direct line of fire, but reducing the bull's speed had enabled Black to all but reach the tree in safety, and it was as he was preparing to jump for it that the bull hooked him from behind and tossed him. The toss landed him on a branch well off the ground. A heavy leather belt he wore had taken the strain when the bull lifted him. The bull was still standing blowing froth from both nostrils when a bullet in the brain terminated proceedings.

The second time a bull did not toss him, but pushed him so deep into a dense cluster of thorn-bush that even the buffalo thought it better to wait for him to extricate himself before doing any more damage. It was as the bull stood waiting for him to emerge from the thorns that I was able to come to his rescue, and it took Black nearly half an hour to disentangle himself from the mass of undergrowth.

The third time was when, in a spirit of bravado, he came too close to a wounded bull lying on the ground. He was going to finish the job by placing a bullet squarely between the eyes— it was as simple as all that. Black was never a great marksman, and instead of placing the bullet between the eyes, he placed it so close to the bull's nose that it threw a lot of dust in its face. Before he had time to fire another shot the bull was on all fours and Black was stepping it out at an incredible speed. It was as the bull was lowering its head for the toss that I managed to place a bullet high on the shoulders and stopped him in his tracks. Black did not turn round to see what the result of my shot was, but kept on running at top speed until he collapsed in a heap as the result of his all-out effort. An hour later Black's hands started to shake violently. Ten years later they were still shaking, and during all that time he had stuck to his resolution never to have any more dealings with buffaloes. It was as a result of this resolution that he was relieved from dangerous hunting and given permanent employment on safer work.

In camp Black's loyalty was never above suspicion. He had three serious weaknesses: women, beer, and a glib tongue. Whenever trouble arose among the native labourers, it could always be traced directly to Black. It was always he who started a movement to demand better wages, more meat, shorter hours, and the numerous agitations one encounters with a native labour staff. When I grew, and cured, my own tobacco, and had five natives whose daily task was to roll 100 cigars each, it was Black who had to supervise the work and check in the daily returns. But it was Black also who sold half the output at less than a penny each, and he it was who instructed the rollers to make him cigars—more than a foot long, with which he impressed his lady friends.

For these lapses I had often beaten him soundly, and on at least a dozen occasions I had fired him and paid him off, with an injunction never to show his face anywhere near me again. Whenever Black got fired he would make for the nearest native kraal, where he would set out on a glorious spree and make merry with the female population. This licentious mode of living would continue as long as his money lasted. After that he would return to work as though nothing unusual had happened.

It was of no use to remonstrate with Black. I was his ' father ', his protector, and he knew of no way in which he could eke out an existence without my help. Black's arithmetic was as faulty as his loyalty, for when the trouble was at its height he would solemnly remind me that he had devoted *fifty* years of his life to me, and that during all that time he had served me truly and loyally. Then there was that occasion when he had saved my life in the bush. By the time Black had finished explaining to me why he considered himself exempt from the sack, I felt that no crime short of murder would justify my dispensing with his services. Shifting Black was like shifting the Rock of Gibraltar.

At the time the conversation I have recorded at the beginning of this chapter took place, I was running a small gold-mine in Rhodesia. A few years before this incident occurred I was acting as compound manager on another gold-mine in Tanganyika, and Black had staged another conversation for my special benefit. It went something like this: ' The compound police on this property are a bad lot; they will see people murdered and buried in the middle of the night without making a report to the compound manager. Perhaps they are afraid to speak, but if it goes on like this we may all soon be murdered and buried without a word being said.'

That conversation set me on the trail which ended in the arrest of four gangsters, two of whom were hanged for murder. Black never appeared in court, nor was his name mentioned in evidence, and there was no need for him to fear reprisals.

But this present conversation intrigued me, and I decided I would call him in to give me more information. Later that night I sent for him and asked him for the details of this get-rich-quick scheme. Yes, the story was perfectly true. The friend to whom he had talked that morning knew someone who knew the spot where one of the wives of the old Matabele king, Lobengula, was buried. The grave contained many ingots of gold and other valuables which were buried with her. But a curse had been put on the grave, and anyone interfering with it was bound to come to a bad end. This friend was willing to take any adventurous European to the spot on condition that he was paid five pounds and that he was not asked to take any active part in stripping the grave.

I felt sceptical about it all and showed little interest in what I believed was a well-thought-out scheme to induce me to part with five pounds. The condition of Black's shoes and clothes was all the incentive required to think up such a scheme; but in the end Black's persistence induced me to change my mind and I asked him to bring along this friend of a friend so that I might obtain more information on the subject.

Late that night there was a knock at my door: Black had brought along the friend who knew all about the grave and the exact spot where it was located. We sat talking for a long time, and in the end it was decided that at midnight the following night we would proceed by car for a distance of roughly 10 miles. From that point to where the grave was— a distance of about 3 miles—we would have to walk through dense bush. Next day I bought a roll of white calico, and Black was left to cut strips which would be tied to trees as markers on the way to the grave. This would help me to find the grave without escort in the day-time.

At sunset that evening everything was prepared for our trip later that night to the grave of the queen, but shortly after dark Black was back on my doorstep. He had come to tell me that all arrangements for the night were cancelled. The guide had reason to believe that he was suspect and being watched. At a later date, when things were quiet and all suspicions allayed, we would start afresh.

Fully a month passed without any further talk about the subject, then Black again appeared outside my door one evening to say that all was in readiness for that night. It was a dark and eerie night, and a heavy drizzle had set in shortly after Black had left me. I felt certain that, in view of the unfavourable conditions, the trip would once again be cancelled.

I had already turned in for the night when there was a knock at my door. The guide was there ready to take me out. The 10 miles by car was completed fairly easily, but from there onwards we were led along a tortuous path through dense forest. Every now and again the guide would stop and listen intently. It was obvious that he was working under great strain and fear. For more than an hour we followed him on that winding path through the dense bush. Black was appointed to the job of tying calico strips to the branches every twenty or thirty paces. It was a few minutes before two o'clock in the morning when we finally came to a stop and the guide pointed to a big tree, the outline of which we could see clearly in the dark.

'Below that tree, Inkos, is the grave,' he said in a whisper. 'It will be well for you to wait for a few days before you come back here; and make sure that no one sees you. I myself will not accompany you, for if it becomes known that I have brought you to this spot, I will be killed without any doubt.'

It was at that moment that the sound of a native drum could be clearly heard in the distance. It was a deliberate beat, and the eeriness of it did not fail to make an impression on me. The guide, who had shown signs of extreme nervousness all night, now went into a panic of fear. To him that sound had an evil portent. He was convinced that someone in the village was aware of what was happening and that the sound of the drum was a death warrant.

For many years previously I had devoted a great deal of time to the study of the African drums, and whereas I cannot interpret messages correctly, I could tell that there was something ominous in that sound. We returned to the waiting car in utter silence, and two hours later I was back in bed, but for the hour or so of remaining darkness I could not sleep, for my mind kept turning to the strange and eerie events in which I had figured in the early hours. Later that afternoon I again discussed the matter with Black, and it was decided that we should proceed to the spot on the following Saturday afternoon —four days later. We would leave fairly late, so that we would arrive at the spot shortly before sunset, when no one was likely to be about.

On the Friday morning I was busy attending to some routine work when Black appeared at the window. He was extremely agitated, and intimated that he wanted to speak to me privately. Once out of earshot, he informed me that the friend with whom I had heard him talking on the first occasion had mysteriously disappeared, and the guide who had taken us out to the grave had been taken seriously ill that morning. He was convinced that the native who had disappeared had been murdered and the body hidden away, and he had no doubt that the man who had taken us out that night had been poisoned and would surely die. Black was in an obvious state of terror, and kept repeating that it would be only a matter of time before he himself would also be effectively put out of the way. He begged me to have no more to do with the business, for fear that I too would come to an untimely end.

I did my best to pacify him and assure him that the missing man would soon return, and that there was no reason to suppose that the guide was suffering from anything more serious than stomach trouble. But nothing I could say would calm him, and when he left me terror was written all over his face. There was such an urgency in all Black had said that I could not help feeling worried myself.

Early next day Black was back at my office again; if anything, he looked much worse than he did the day before. He had come to inform me that the guide had died during the night, and that there was still no sign of the missing man. Nothing could persuade him that he himself was not booked for a similar fate. He pleaded with me again to have nothing more to do with the business.

Next morning Black sent word to say that he was too ill to come to work; I immediately went to see him, and he assured me that 'they' had caught up with him too. A doctor was soon in attendance, and I told him that I suspected foul play. Black was subjected to a thorough examination and was visited twice more that day by the doctor, but by nightfall it was obvious that he was beyond all help. The last conscious word he spoke to me was to warn me never to go near that grave again. Shortly after that he passed away. I arranged for a post-mortem to be held, but apart from the many normal ailments from which almost every African native suffers, nothing definite was ever discovered.

A few days after Black was buried I again drove to the spot where we had left the car that night. For an hour or more I searched for the strips we had tied to the trees to mark the way to the grave; there was not a trace of one to be seen anywhere, and of the thousands of trees in that area, it was quite impossible for me to identify one of which I had seen only the outline on that fateful night.

As far as I know, there was no post-mortem on the native who died so suddenly, and the native who disappeared so mysteriously has never been seen again, and this in spite of an intensive search by his relatives and friends. In my own mind there is no doubt that the moment it was discovered that they were concerned in an effort to open the grave, steps were taken to have them removed. I had it on good authority that Black and the guide were not the first to pay with their lives for trying to interfere with that grave, and knowing this, it is unlikely that any other native who knows the exact spot where the grave is located, will take the risk of bringing upon himself the vengeance of those who watch. Perhaps some other bold adventurer may have better luck than I had and with less serious consequences than attended my effort.

CHAPTER XX

THE WHITE FATHERS

IF THERE IS a finer, more human, body of men anywhere in the world than the Catholic White Fathers brotherhood in Tanganyika, I should love to meet them. During my last fifteen years in the bush in Central Africa I was in almost daily contact with the Fathers of one mission or another, and although I do not belong to the Catholic faith, this fact made no difference whatever to the deep and close friendship that grew up between us.

When I was in charge of supplies on a big mine in the Uru-wira district in Northern Tanganyika during the last war, I was often able to assist the Fathers with items of every-day necessity which, owing to their complete isolation and difficult transport problems in such an out-of-the-way corner of the world, they were otherwise unable to obtain. During the whole of the period I spent on this property all foodstuffs, drinks, and smokes, and even medical supplies, were strictly rationed, and were obtained exclusively for the staff. Now that it is all over, and I am well beyond their reach, the staff of the organization will understand why hardly a week ever passed without a considerable share of their rations being in ' short supply '.

When finally I left the property, the mission paid me a compliment which I shall always cherish as one of the happiest memories of my bush life. On this occasion the Bishop of the order, who was stationed at Ujiji, many hundreds of miles to the north, made a special trip to be present to witness my departure.

But my help to them was by no means a one-way traffic. Whenever the Fathers could assist me in any way, they were always only too pleased and happy to do so. Thus it was with their assistance and advice that I learned how to ferment and distil honey and make the finest ' moonshine ' ever produced in Tanganyika.

They also provided me with seeds and taught me how to

grow, and cure, my own tobacco and roll my own cigars. My first year's two-acre crop produced no less than 10,000 cigars and, although cigarettes and tobacco were strictly rationed, I cannot remember ever starting a safari without each native porter being issued with a liberal supply of cigars. Sitting around the camp-fires at night, it was an incongruous sight to see natives, barefooted, dressed in tattered rags, unwashed and unkempt, discussing the day's doings with fat cigars between their teeth.

The distilling business also had its humorous side. In a short while I was producing an excellent selection of home-made liqueurs. The moonshine itself was a potent and power-ful product. Put through the still three times made it a three-star liquor; five times was a five-star product which had the kick of a mule. My greatest difficulty was to find a native who could be trusted to watch the fires in the distilling process and make sure that the brew was not overheated. A steady drip—drop for drop—ensured a safe product; overheating created fusel oil, which is harmful. A fairly safe test was to pour some of the liquid into a saucer and set it alight. A red flame would indicate the presence of fusel, and the brew would have to be re-stilled. A blue flame indicated that it was reasonably safe to drink. Black, my old headman, generally took charge of the fires, but I often came home in the after-noons to find him stretched out in a drunken stupor, and a whole pot of brew spoiled. Black, on these occasions, always maintained that the fumes had overcome him. On one occasion the fumes were so potent that it took him all day to crawl to his hut, less than 100 yards away.

At that time there were some fifty Europeans employed on the property, and the still became a community affair. Each member of the staff contributed his share to purchase the ' raw material '—honey, which we bought at six shillings for four gallons—and the product was equally divided. Four gallons of honey would produce something like twenty bottles of plus 90 degree alcohol, which brought the cost to roughly three pennies per bottle. The raw taste was to a large extent eliminated by putting orange-peel in the bottles, which gave it a flavour of vodka. In spite of war conditions and the strict rationing, the tobacco and drink question was effectively solved, and things went along merrily, until news came through one morning that the District Commissioner was on his way to the property on a tour of inspection.

An unregistered still, operating in a mining camp, would be one of the first things to come under official notice; a first offence carried with it a fine of £150 or six months in the house of correction. I decided to dismantle the installation and hide all the evidence as best I could before the official put in an appearance. In order to avoid any awkward questions, I decided I would go on a week's hunting safari early the next morning and keep out of the way until all danger had passed.

That night my truck was loaded, and it only remained to collect the necessary prophylactics and camp medicines from the dispensary early the next morning. The dispensary usually opened at 7 a.m., and just before that hour I was on my way to collect the medicines. As I walked along the path I noticed a stranger strolling up and down the veranda of the dispensary. I was about to slide in at the door when he called me over. 'You are Mr. Burger?' he queried. On admitting that I was, he continued, 'I'm the District Commissioner. I believe you are brewing hooch in the camp.'

The blow had fallen!

I was still thinking of something to say in defence of myself when he continued, 'And I believe it is very good stuff too; have you a bottle you can spare?'

After some discussion it was agreed that I should send him five bottles of assorted liqueurs and a bottle of my special five star. The bottles were to be labelled 'Flit', Dip, Disinfectant, etc., etc. 'Flit' represented the five star. The order was duly attended to, and later that morning I left on my safari. Only then did it begin to dawn on me that I had actually supplied all the evidence to land me in serious trouble. The thought remained with me until my return ten days later. Back in the office I found a telegram waiting for me.

On opening it I read: 'Send urgently two bottles flit and any available disinfectants. D.C.'

The flit and other available disinfectants were duly supplied; in fact, supplies were sent regularly until I left the property several months later. It was with great sorrow that I heard a few years later that this genial official had died suddenly of heart failure. He was by that time no longer in the service.

When I left the property some nine months later, I decided I would go on a six months' hunting safari in the Rift Valley. The still was once more dismantled and taken on safari with me. For two months I camped with the White Fathers at Mamba Mission—one of the beauty spots in Tanganyika. The still was again installed, and supplied the local requirements. My technique in distilling and preparing choice liqueurs improved rapidly under expert guidance, and all the missions in that part of Tanganyika were generously supplied with the local product.

It was whilst I was at Mamba Mission that the Father Superior asked me to go down to Cherida to attend to a killer buffalo bull. This bull had caused a great deal of trouble, and on several occasions natives on their way with supplies to the Mission had been treed and kept there for hours whilst the brute menaced them from below. The trip should have lasted only two days, but at the end of four days I was still trailing the bull without success. By that time my larder was completely depleted, and it was a happy sight when I returned empty-handed to camp late one afternoon, footsore, hungry, and completely discouraged, to find a sumptuous spread of food—cakes, milk, cheese, etc., etc.—awaiting me. The Fathers had heard from passing natives of the trouble I was having in getting the bull under fire. One of them had immediately packed a basket of provisions, and cycled 30 miles on a motor-bike, over impossible roads, to bring supplies to me. That bull was eventually accounted for in strange circumstances which I have related elsewhere.

Shortly after I returned to the Mission from this safari I joined the Red Locust Control Organization. This was at the end of November. Whilst I was busy one morning dismantling my camp, the Father Superior called on me. He had come to tell me how sorry they all were that I was leaving the Mission and also to inquire what I intended doing with the still. I had no intention of carrying such a cumbersome installation with me into the bush, and I had already decided to present the Mission with it. The Father was very pleased with the idea, but insisted that I accept payment for it. I told him that I would in no circumstances accept money from him, and that the still was a gift in appreciation of the many kindnesses I had received from them. Fairly soon after it had been delivered at the Mission, a native porter arrived at my camp with a cardboard package. On opening the package I found it to contain an almost new portable typewriter—a gift from the Father Superior of the Mission. That typewriter has now given me ten years' service. It was used to type the scripts of my previous book *African Buffalo Trails* and is being used now to type these scripts. I can only hope that the still has given equally good service.

This was not to be the last welcome gift from the Mission. After I joined the Locust Control staff I was posted to a camp more than 100 miles away from the Mission. During the entire nine months I spent on Control work I was accompanied by my wife, Doris. It came to Christmas Eve, and we were sitting on a little sand dune miles out in the Rift Valley. The entire surrounding country had been flooded for weeks owing to the heavy rains. Our larder had reached the stage where even the barest necessities were running dangerously low, and there was absolutely nothing with which to celebrate Christmas. In such circumstances life in the bush can be very grim. That night we sat for a long time bemoaning our lot and soundly denouncing the transport system which had failed so dismally and landed us in our present predicament. The only consolation we had was that there was still sufficient food to prevent us from starving to death on Christmas Day. It was a cheerless outlook indeed.

Early on Christmas morning I left camp to see what I could do to provide the labourers with game meat for the day. I had previously promised them that for Christmas I would try to give them as much meat as they could eat—a big order when dealing with 300 natives. It was just on ten o'clock that morning before I had succeeded in shooting enough game to keep them happy, and when I returned to camp shortly before mid-day, it was to find Doris in a state of great excitement and happiness. Soon after I left camp that morning a native messenger on a cycle had arrived from Mamba Mission. He had brought with him another cardboard box. This time it was packed with Christmas pudding, cakes, sweets, ham, sausages, fruit, and other delicacies; in addition, there was an excellent selection of products from the still. It was just one more kindly thought which meant so much to us and helped to make our Christmas a cheerful one.

On our return from the campaign we called once again at Mamba Mission and spent a happy week there. We were deeply distressed to hear that the Father Superior had left for Holland only a few weeks earlier in order to undergo a serious operation on his eyes. At the time of his departure he was almost completely blind. More than a year later, after I had returned to Southern Rhodesia, a letter arrived for me from Holland. It was from the Father, and carried the glad tidings that the operation had been a complete success and that he was shortly going back to Africa.

CHAPTER XXI

AFRICAN DRUMS

'The drums are speaking early tonight. The villagers down in the valley are anxious to know what we are up to, and the drummer up on the hill has been telling them that they have nothing to fear. Just now he is telling them that we have supplied them with a lot of meat today.'

Muke, the speaker, was one of my gun-bearers, and as he had done on several previous occasions, he was interpreting the messages coming in and going out. Up to now I had had no conclusive proof that Muke could, in fact, interpret messages in as full detail as he would have me believe, but tonight the situation was different, and I fervently hoped that he could read those messages correctly. We were sitting round the camp-fire in Ubangi, right in the heart of the cannibal country.

It was only a couple of days earlier that I had come to realize that we were deep in cannibal country and that we were treading on extremely dangerous ground. Since making the startling discovery I had guards posted out every night, fearing as I did that we might be attacked unexpectedly at any time and turned into stew. When one listens to the drums under such conditions one's nerves become strained and one is apt to be fearful, for one never knows what the purport of a message may be. I had known for many years that the drums could rap out messages with great detail and that such messages could be correctly interpreted. But, like so many other Europeans, I had tried and failed to interpret the drums. The best I could do was to tell the general tenor of a message. When danger and intrigue threaten, the drums carry out an eerie, long-drawn-out beat which is alternated frequently with rapid, short, loud beats. Happier moods are transmitted in a totally different and more regular rhythm.

Muke was a native from Northern Rhodesia and could not speak the language of the inhabitants of the Ubangi, but he assured me that the messages are all the same in all native languages and that he did not find it difficult to read the local drums. It is quite a common thing for natives to read messages in their own country—a fact I had often proved before, but I was not at all satisfied that Muke could correctly interpret the messages in a country where he was a stranger and where the language was foreign to him. In spite of his definite assurance that all was well, I again posted guards that night and hoped for the best.

Late the following afternoon we arrived at the village which had received the messages of our movements the previous night. The villagers were well aware of all we had done and knew every detail of our safari: the number of guns we carried, details of the game we had killed during the past few days, and even the number of foreign natives I had in my safari. These facts I ascertained through an interpreter I had brought with me. It is true the information the villagers had about us might have been carried ahead of our safari by a local messenger, and I felt that this would explain more satisfactorily the complete knowledge they had about our movements. At all events, their comprehensive knowledge, allegedly transmitted by drums, in no way proved that Muke could likewise read the drums and I remained sceptical—and worried.

That night the drums were busy again, and as on the previous night Muke was again interpreting. Among other things, he told me that the drummer sending messages from the next village had stated that there had been an accident in the bush that day. A man had been mauled by a wild animal—he was not certain what kind of animal—the villagers were convinced that the man would not recover from his injuries and that he would undoubtedly die.

We did not leave the village the following day, the headman having asked me to shoot some game for his people, but the day after we were on our way early in the morning. When we arrived at the next village after dark that night, one of the first things I learned was that a man had died that morning as a result of having been mauled by a lion two days earlier. Here again the information in the first place may have been carried to the kraal where Muke took the message that evening. On checking up, however, I found that the accident had taken place shortly before sunset—about 6.30 p.m. It was not later than 8 p.m. that night when Muke gave me the information. Obviously no messenger could have travelled over 20 miles on foot in a matter of ninety minutes.

For the rest of the trip through the Ubangi I depended on Muke nightly to interpret the messages, and throughout the trip I was able to check up regularly. There were occasions when minor details were incorrectly interpreted, but in general I was kept well advised as to what was happening around us all the time, and it was largely due to Muke's ability to interpret messages correctly that I was able to complete that safari through the most hostile and savage country in Central Africa without any serious untoward incident.

Just to what extent natives can interpret messages has always been a controversial matter. A few years ago the late ex D.C. Chadwick entered into an acrimonious dispute with a well-known philologist who had come out to Africa to study drum communications from a scientific point of view. His final decision was that the whole business was imaginary, and he gave several reasons why he considered reliable transmission to be beyond the powers of native drummers—especially in cases where languages were dissimilar. How thoroughly he went into the question, and what opportunities he had of seeing expert drummers at work, I do not know; but Chadwick had had a life-long experience in the African bush, and whereas he did not approach the subject from a scientific point of view, he certainly had his own practical experience to fall back on, and he quoted numerous cases where he had seen messages interpreted which could have been communicated by no other method but the drums. The discussion took up quite a lot of space in one of the popular South African papers and closed with both men sticking to their views. For my part, I am firmly convinced that messages with great detail can be sent and interpreted in Central Africa—if nowhere else.

It was some years after this safari through the Ubangi that Muke was once again put to the test, and I was given a practical demonstration that drum communication is a positive reality. At that time I was running a Talkie Cinema in Jadotville, Belgian Congo; that was right at the beginning of the advent of the Talkies. Muke had then been with me for many years; an intelligent native, he had been taught to

N

operate one of the projectors.   On this occasion we were showing a Martin Johnson film, ' Congorilla '.   I was standing
next to Muke in the operator's cabin, watching the first re-
hearsal of the film.   Suddenly there was an interlude of drum-
beating.   Muke immediately started to interpret the message
for me.   A few seconds later the text was repeated by the
commentator of the film; it was almost identical with the
version Muke had given me.

Whilst the Chadwick argument was appearing in print I
often felt tempted to enter the lists on his side with this indis-
putable proof of the reality of communication by drums, but he
was doing quite well on his own account, and I left it at that.
Just how natives of different tribes and speaking different
languages are yet able to interpret messages is something I am
quite unable to explain; but the fact is that they do, and to the
wanderer in the wilds, especially at the time and in the
locality of which I write, the drums can be a nerve-wrecking
business.   Not every wanderer in those days had the advantage of having a reliable interpreter at his disposal.   I feel
convinced that if Dickson, whose murder I have described
elsewhere, had had the advantage of a reliable interpreter
during his ill-fated trip through the Ubangi, he would never
have entered that village of ill repute.

It is not only in the matter of beating out messages on drums
that natives in the back-blocks of Africa perform extraordinary
and inexplicable feats.   Many of the strange things they do
can be attributed to clever trickery and a play on the fear of
witchcraft and superstition.   Others again cannot be explained
in this manner.   How must one explain the strange apparition
of a hyena skin coming to life, baring its fangs and menacing
squatters round the camp-fire at night when, in fact, there is
no hyena at all?   It is true magicians and sleight-of-hand
merchants the world over can perform stranger feats than this,
but they have the advantages of hall, distance, trappings, and
lighting effects to help them.

To sit round the camp-fire at night, out in the far back-
blocks of Africa, and see a native appear in tattered clothes,
with a few skins, beads, and bones round his body for adorn-
ment, squat near the fire, deposit a hyena skin, start a quaint
chant, and before your eyes bring the skin to life and induce it

to go through all the antics of a live beast, is something alto-
gether different. Mass hypnotism, I have been told, will
explain it. That may be true. I know nothing about
hypnotism—except the type used by the Income Tax Department—but how does a raw native out in the wilds learn to
hypnotize a large audience sitting in semi-darkness round a
camp-fire at night?

How does one explain the '*fundi*' who claims that he has
inside him a spirit that controls the most vicious and loath-
some of all insects—the scorpion? Time and again I have seen
' Scorpion Men ' uncover a nest of the brutes—some of them
fully 8 inches long—pick them up in their bare hands, and
place them inside their shirts next to their naked bodies without
a sting ever resulting! Black had the answer for that one:
he was quite certain that, by a quick movement, not percep-
tible to the onlooker, the scorpions were deprived of their stings.
It was as simple as all that. But when the *fundi* pulled a
scorpion out from his shirt and placed it in Black's hand, I
quickly had to resort to permanganate of potash treatment to
stop him from yelling the roof down.

In spite of their daily close contact with insects and reptiles,
it is extremely rare for natives to learn which are poisonous and
which are harmless species. I have yet to see a native who is
not scared stiff of a chameleon, and without exception they will
tell you that there is no cure for a chameleon bite.

With snakes it is the same. Every snake is ' deadly poisonous ', and it is here where the tricksters come to light. In the
few rare cases where they have learned to recognize harmless
snakes they will make great play and claim supernatural
powers. Often the knowledge is used to cash in at the expense
of the ignorant.

Up in the Uruwira district I once watched a ' snake man '
taking a collection from spectators. In his enclosure he had a
large collection of harmless grass snakes and mole snakes, and
these he handled with complete indifference and often took
bites from them, to the horror and astonishment of the onlookers. There were many cobras and puff-adders in this
district, but these species were absent from the snake-man's
collection. I determined I would have some fun with this
fraud and expose him.

The next Sunday he was again giving a performance and taking a collection. I had in the meanwhile collected a puff-adder, which I brought along in a closed box. During the performance I entered the enclosure and picked up a few of the grass snakes and allowed them to crawl round my neck. The performance was received with great acclamation, and I was forthwith accepted as a '*fundi*'.

A few moments later I left the enclosure and emptied the box containing the puff-adder quite close to where the ' snake man ' stood. The leap that took him over that five-feet-high enclosure was a classical demonstration of the effortless high jump.

On another occasion, however, the joke was against me, and might have ended disastrously. One of the local snake-men was again performing outside my tent. In response to loud laughter and cheering, I went out to see what it was all about.

I was amused to see my wife, Doris, holding a snake by the head and tail, and frightening the onlookers with it. For a moment I believed that it was a harmless grass snake, but something about the appearance of the reptile struck me as unfamiliar in a grass snake; on closer examination I was horrified to find that it was a deadly cobra she was holding. A variation in colour had induced the snake-man to believe that it was a harmless snake, and he had handed it to her. It was with some effort that I managed to keep calm until I had relieved her of that package.

CHAPTER XXII

STRANGE CHARACTERS

A few months before his death, my old friend, Micky Norton, called on me one day whilst I was sitting checking over some manuscripts. During the course of casual conversation I mentioned to him that I intended one day to write about some of the strange characters I had met during my wanderings in Central Africa, and that he himself would figure prominently on the list. Micky's rejoinder was to the effect that if I intended to write about strange characters I would do well to forget about others and write about myself instead.

I have never considered that there is anything very strange about me, but perhaps I lack the gift Bobby Burns prayed for —the gift to see ourselves as others see us. So far as I know, the main reason why Micky considered me strange was because I persistently showed a preference for hunting buffaloes and always deplored the fact that elephants should be hunted for profit. When an elephant turned vagabond or caused damage by destroying crops or property, it did not disturb me so much to shoot the culprit; but when it came to a question of hunting them for their ivory, I always felt distressed to think that such a noble, intelligent animal, with his enormous bulk and normally placid nature, should be killed in order to improve the hunter's financial position.

I cannot remember a single occasion, even when necessity dictated the killing, that I have walked up to the carcass of a dead elephant without feeling a sense of guilt. The feeling often remained with me for days, and this I do not attribute to squeamishness. When one hunts for a living there is little room for squeamishness—but in the case of elephant my conscience always registered a protest.

Micky had quite different views on the subject, and contended that even a sparrow valued its life as highly as an elephant, and he could see no reason why size and bulk should ensure immunity for any animal. Perhaps he was right, and my unconventional views must have appeared 'strange' to him. But that, in itself, is not sufficient inducement or justification for writing a book on the subject, and in spite of Micky's assertion, I still think that many other strange characters can with advantage hold the stage for a fleeting moment. Their strange behaviour, and still stranger outlook on life, never failed to intrigue and amuse me, and I feel that at least one or two will prove of interest and amusement to the reader.

There was Bish, who once fell foul of a big elephant bull which he had wounded with the only rifle he had at his disposal at the moment—an antiquated old model .303 service rifle which, I believe, had seen service in the Boer War some thirty years earlier. Bish was lucky that the shooting took place near what must have been the highest and steepest anthill in the Belgian Congo. By the time the bull reached the foot of the anthill Bish had already crept to the very top. The anthill was too steep for the elephant to negotiate, and Bish, now comfortably seated well out of reach of the infuriated bull, proceeded to pump lead into the beast, and it was the twelfth shot that finally brought it to its knees. By that time the bull had already negotiated more than half the anthill, and Bish's position had become extremely precarious.

There is nothing remarkable about this exploit—to be driven up a tree or anthill is a normal everyday occurrence in the hunting game—but what was remarkable about it was that the bull was found to carry the second largest pair of tusks ever recorded up to that time, measuring 9 feet 3 inches and weighing 195 lb. and 197 lb. respectively. With ivory at twenty-two shillings per lb., as it was then, Bish was amply rewarded for his hectic experience on the top of that anthill.

His native gun-bearer, who carried the heavy elephant rifle, had seen the trouble start from a safe distance, and came rushing into my camp some time afterwards to report that the bull had surely killed Bish. When I reached the spot a little later, Bish was far from dead; he was, in fact, busy measuring the tusks of his trophy. That was not the only occasion on which Bish was reported dead to me. It happened on at least half a dozen other occasions. The last time, before he eventually died, was when I was working alluvial gold on the Sira River in Tanganyika. Later that afternoon I received a report that Bish had died that morning in the Chunya hospital, and would be buried the following day. At that time I had known him for more than twenty years and had shared many safaris with him.

Although the cemetery where he was to be buried was more than 20 miles from my camp, I decided I would walk that distance in order to pay my last respects to him. At daybreak next morning I was on my way to Chunya, where the funeral was due to take place that afternoon. After I had walked all of 12 miles, the vanguard of a safari coming in my direction could be seen in the distance. A few minutes later I was face to face with the leader of the safari—it was my old friend Bish. He stoutly denied that he had died the previous day. It was no use disputing the fact—the evidence was there staring me in the face. On this occasion it was a namesake of his who had died.

Bish it was who successfully shot up two police camps in the Belgian Congo. The trouble was that the officers would not see eye to eye with him in the matter of illicit elephant-hunting. For this exploit he was sentenced to three months' imprisonment, but he became so troublesome that in the end he was released, after serving three weeks of his sentence. He it was also who stuffed thirty kilos of gold, worth over £3,000, in the frame of his bicycle, which he left in the store-room of a police office for safe keeping. The gold was illicitly bought, and the officer in whose care the bicycle was left was at that moment making inquiries and looking for evidence to convict Bish. The evidence he required was just one piece of the gold lying in his storeroom.

But it was not only in these incongruous situations that Bish provided the humour. I was with him one day when he was working in an unventilated room with a gang of natives. In a short while the odour of human bodies had become so strong that he had to rush out for fresh air. On reaching the door he remarked to me, ' I cannot understand these black beasts. Now I myself, I have a bath once a month, whether I need it or not, but these black b——s never bathe at all '! Bish had actually described the position correctly: a bath was strictly a monthly feature with him. The next time I received news that Bish had passed on, the report was unfortunately true, but on that occasion I was many hundreds of miles away and could not pay my last respects to him.

Another strange character whose fluctuations of fortune affected me very closely was Rosie.   He succeeded in securing a lucrative sanitary contract in the Congo.   Ten natives were employed on the job, and all went well for some time, until one night Rosie decided to absent himself from work and leave the gang to carry on whilst he did a tour of the cafés.   The staff must have thought that what was good for the goose was also good for the gander, and no work was done that night. Rosie, however, determined that it was not going to be quite so good for the gander.

When rations were issued that afternoon he showed his disapproval by mixing a strong dose of cyanide with each ration. This exploit landed him in serious trouble, for four of the natives died.   At his trial he was found guilty of ' multiple murder ' and attempted murder, and was sentenced to fifteen years' imprisonment.   At the time of sentence, however, it was pointed out to him that, being a first offender, he was entitled to write to the King of the Belgians and ask for forgiveness.   In due course Rosie was forgiven and set free.

It was shortly after his release that he came to me with a million-franc scheme which could not possibly miscarry.   My contribution to make the scheme a success was to be 5,000 francs.   With that amount of money he could cultivate and raise a million *porros* (leeks) on a plot he owned out of town. *Porros* were then selling at a franc a piece, and that was how the million-franc figure was arrived at—it was as simple as all that—and I parted with 5,000 francs.   The crop, I was assured, would be ready for sale in under four months.

It was quite six months before I saw Rosie again; he had then come to borrow twenty francs from me in order to buy *porros* on the morning market for his own use.   Somewhere along the line the million-franc enterprise had come to grief. The story was so involved that I still do not know just what happened.   When some time later he again called on me to offer me a thirty-acre plot of ground near Jadotville for 10,000 francs, I felt suspicious, in spite of his definite assurance that in time the ground would be worth more than a million francs—Rosie always counted in millions.   The *porro* deal was still rankling in my mind and I did not feel disposed to be taken in for another 10,000. But in the end Rosie's persistence prevailed, and I agreed to buy the property on condition that the deeds of transfer were approved officially in Elisabethville. That same night Rosie left for Elisabethville to have the transfer legalized, but on his way down he got himself mixed up in a brawl, during which he was thrown out of the train. His body was picked up by a ganger the next day.

With the death of Rosie I lost all further interest in the deal, and the property was sold with the rest of his estate. I had cause for serious regret three years later, when that particular piece of land was sold for one and half million francs. The area had become the centre of a vast expansion programme, and the ground was divided into small plots and sold in the open market. On making inquiries, I was offered a half-acre plot for 50,000 francs; the franc at that time stood at 120 to the pound sterling.

There was Charlie, who grew the finest and longest beard I ever saw on any man. It reached down to his waist and gave him the appearance of a character right out of the Old Testament. Charlie was justly proud of that beard, for on at least two occasions—so the story goes—it helped to save his life.

The first time was when, after a convivial evening in Kungutas, he set out on his way to his camp, 5 miles down the Lupa River. All along the banks of the river the grass grew 10 feet high and the path that wound its way through this morass was not much more than a foot wide. Charlie had walked this path without untoward incident on scores of occasions previously, and as usual he carried a small hurricane lamp to light the way. He was making good progress until he reached a sharp bend in the path. As he took the bend he came face to face with a huge male lion travelling in the opposite direction, on the same path. This unexpected encounter brought both man and beast to a sudden stop.

In this desperate position, and for something better to do or say, he yelled out at the top of his voice, ' Hop it, you skunk; hop it! ' The lion looked at him for a tense moment or two and then quickly disappeared in the long grass. Charlie always maintained that it was the beard, and not the insult he hurled at the lion, that was responsible for its sudden flight.

In the beginning no one believed Charlie's story—the general opinion was that he had seen a stray dog—but a week later the lion was shot at a camp quite close to where Charlie had met it that night.

The next time the beard—or what was left of it—came to his rescue was when a practical joker had found him fast asleep in a drunken stupor on a bench outside an hotel. When he awoke it was to find himself deprived of the beard all along one side of his face. Deeply offended at the indignity inflicted upon him, he forthwith set off on his way home. The river at the time of the year was in flood, and whilst crossing a narrow bridge he missed his footing and fell into the torrent below. It was whilst he was making frantic efforts to reach the banks that a passing native heard his screams. A rescue was finally effected when the native managed to get hold of the remaining section of his beard and haul him to safety. But the evil day was only deferred for a few months, when he again missed his footing, but on this occasion there was no one near to pull him by the beard, and his body was found the following day a mile down the stream.

Then there was Dave Le Page, who set the headlines of the world press ablaze with the news that he had discovered a Brontosaurus in the forest in the Belgian Congo; readers may remember this incident. What Dave had actually seen that day was an outsize hippo bull—a fact of which he was fully aware—but the Belgian journalist who accompanied him on that occasion had never previously seen a Brontosaurus or a hippo of that size, and Dave firmly convinced him that the animal which had rushed past them in that overgrown swamp was a Brontosaurus—an animal that became extinct some million years ago. For some weeks not only the journalist, but thousands of people all over the world, believed that there was actually a live Brontosaurus running about in the bush not far from Elisabethville. The *Essor du Congo*—the Belgian newspaper that was responsible for sending out the report—was inundated with inquiries from almost every country for weeks after the announcement first appeared. I was camped quite close to Dave when all this happened, and enjoyed the joke to the full.

Several years later I again met him in Tanganyika Territory, where he was then prospecting for gold. Late one afternoon he came to my camp and told me he had found the largest and richest reef ever discovered in Tanganyika. For a while I believed that he was trying on another joke, but I changed my mind when he pulled out his prospecting bags and threw several handsful of almost pure gold quartz on my table. Laboratory assays subsequently showed that the samples carried over 5 oz. of gold to the ton. I tried hard to find out from him where the reef was located, but Dave was much too wise to divulge this information. Shortly after that he left for the South to raise funds to exploit the property. A fortnight after he left I received the news that he had died suddenly. I spent many weary months in the district searching for the reef, but never found a trace of it. The secret of the whereabouts of that fabulous reef died with Dave. Towards the end of last year it was reported from Tanganyika that a reef carrying up to 15 oz. per ton had been discovered by two prospectors. I have often wondered whether they had better luck than I did in finding Dave's lucky strike.

CHAPTER XXIII

IN MEMORY OF DORIS

Is it not strange how small and unimportant events can sometimes change one's entire life and future? When I was employed as secretary and general factotum on a gold-mine in Tanganyika Territory a great deal of my time was frequently taken up in settling staff troubles and pouring oil on troubled waters.

On one occasion a foreman miner failed to see eye to eye with the chief engineer and walked off the job. Later in the day he sent me a note asking me to prepare his pay cheque, as he had decided to quit for good. The man in question was employed on a job in which it would have been very difficult for us to replace him, and at best it would have taken more time than we could afford. After a round-table conference in the manager's office, it was decided that I should go over to his house and try to patch up the trouble. Apart from everyday routine matters which he often came to discuss in my office, I had had very little to do with the man previously and had not visited his house before. After I had stopped work that afternoon, I decided that I would call on him to endeavour to get matters straightened out.

In response to my knock the door was opened by a youngish, good-looking woman, who invited me in. After I had explained to her the object of my visit she told me that her husband had gone to the nearby town and would be back a little later. We sat talking for an hour or so, at the end of which time the husband had not returned. I decided that I would call later in the evening to see him.

As I reached the door on my way out my attention was drawn to the picture of a beautiful woman, hanging on the wall. The face was so strikingly beautiful that I stood looking at it intently for a minute or two.

' Does she intrigue you? ' I heard my hostess say.

' Yes,' I replied; ' she is extraordinarily beautiful. Who is she? '

' That,' she replied, ' is Doris, my sister. Beautiful, as you say, but that is not the only gift with which the gods have blessed her. She is a great musician—perhaps the finest pianist in all Africa today.'

' To have two such outstanding gifts granted you is a fortune the gods bestow only on those they love,' I replied.

We stood talking for a few minutes longer and she told me that her sister was married and was a concert artist in Johannesburg. Later that night I again called at the house. The husband had returned, and after a long-drawn-out discussion, I finally persuaded him to come back to work. It was a simple everyday occurrence for me to settle such disputes, and all that was different in this case was that after that night I became very friendly with the couple and frequently called on them for sundowners and music, which was provided by a gramophone and an excellent selection of records which we had between us. Hardly a night passed without Doris becoming the topic of conversation, during which her praises were extolled. Before long I began to feel that I had known Doris for many years.

Some months later I became interested in a unique breed of dog which could not be procured in Tanganyika. I mentioned this to Phyllis, my hostess, and she assured me that I would have no difficulty in obtaining one in Johannesburg, where they were being used with great success by the police in tracking down criminals. She suggested that I write to Doris and ask her if she could assist me in the matter. A few days later a letter was posted to her. Apart from my desire to obtain the dog, I felt that it would be interesting to contact a person of whom I had heard so much. It was a fortnight later that I received a reply giving me details of the price of the dog and the best method of having it sent up to Tanganyika.

At that time I frequently contributed articles to one of the Johannesburg newspapers, dealing with Abyssinia, Wild Life in Africa, etc., etc. Doris mentioned in her letter that they had read a recent article I had contributed, and found it of great interest to them. She asked many questions about bush life, and especially animals, of which she was apparently very fond. Answering questions, and writing about bush adventures, soon resulted in regular correspondence between us.

Early one afternoon I received a note from Phyllis asking me not to fail to call on her on my way home after work that afternoon.   When I called later in the day, she handed me a telegram; it was from Doris.   It stated that her husband, who was an internationally famous violinist, had died suddenly from heart failure that morning.   A few days later I received a letter from Doris telling me all about the sad event.   She was deeply grieved, and mentioned that, with the death of her husband, she had decided to discontinue concert work for at least a year, if not for good.

In a subsequent letter to her sister she stated that, with the changed conditions, Johannesburg had become unbearable for her.   She wanted to get away from it all to try to forget.   We discussed the matter that night, and it was decided to invite Doris to come up to Tanganyika and spend some time with her sister.   It was one morning just two months later that she arrived at the mine.   By that time we felt that we were no longer strangers, in spite of the fact that we had not met before. We had much in common: her love of nature, the bush, the animals.   Even snakes and insects never failed to arouse her interest, and, above all, there was our mutual love of good music to bring us closer together.   Her visit was due to last for only three months, but the life in the open spaces, and the numerous safaris to see wild life in its natural state, had made such an appeal to her that she decided to prolong her stay for another three months.

One of my great shortcomings is that there is very little of the romantic in me.   My life of adventure previously had left little room for romance, and I did not think that my mode of living would ever change.   For the next three months life went on happily and placidly enough.   By the end of that time Doris and I had become inseparable companions, and the feeling of friendship had already changed to something much deeper. After three more months had passed the entire programme was revised, for we had decided to be married two months later.   That seemingly unimportant duty I fulfilled that night in persuading a determined miner to change his mind, had turned out to be instrumental in changing my whole future.   It had brought me a beautiful and talented woman who for the next fifteen years loyally devoted her whole life to me and brought me nothing but joy and great happiness.

Before we were married I often sat at night and turned things over in my mind. How would it work out in the end to bring to the bush a woman who, all her life, had been accustomed to the footlights, whose amazing talents had won her the acclaim of packed audiences all over Europe, England, and South Africa? The newness of it all for the previous eight months quite understandably appealed to her. But how long would it be before she would again hanker after that other life of public admiration and acclaim? In the bush there would be no opportunities for her to continue her career. Since I had met her eight months previously I had not even had the opportunity to hear her play, for there was no piano available in that part of the world. But this situation was soon to change, for it became obvious to me that, although she had solemnly assured me that she would *never* again play in public, she was completely lost without a piano in the home. It was time for me to start my apprenticeship in a new business—the business of providing a new piano each time the previous one had been played to a standstill.

During the next fifteen years this happened on eight occasions. The first was an enormous Concert Grand Ibach, which I imported from the South. It was a memorable day when a gang of thirty porters arrived with that piano, which they had carried for more than 20 miles over sodden roads. It was memorable also in so far as I am concerned, for it was the first time that it had ever happened to me to sit miles out in the bush and listen to a great artist render Chopin and the other masters to perfection.

Climatic conditions, especially during the rainy season in Tanganyika, played havoc with the instruments, and they frequently went out of tune. It was difficult enough to procure replacements—finding someone who could keep them in tune presented an even greater problem. But fate was kind. After many inquiries I learned that there was an old digger on the field, eking out a miserable existence, who was a London-trained tuner. He was then well in his seventies and operated a claim some 50 miles from us.

The next day Doris and I went to interview Bill to try to

persuade him to attend to the instrument. Bill's financial position at that time had reached rock bottom, and we had no difficulty in bringing him back home with us. The piano was duly re-tuned. Bill was undoubtedly a first-class craftsman, in spite of his advanced age, but when during the next month I had to bring him back again on four occasions, it began to dawn on me that quite half of my life would be spent in carrying Bill about, to and fro, in the back-blocks of Central Africa.

The difficulty was overcome when I built a good comfortable hut for him near our home and took in as one of the family. He lived with us until his death five years later. By then he had ministered to three different pianos—' She hammers them to pieces in no time,' Bill would complain—and had made Doris self-reliant by teaching her to do her own tuning and repairs. On his death Bill left her his complete tuning equipment, and from then onwards her time was divided equally between playing and ' running repairs ', which had by now become an obsession. One day she would play Chopin and the piano would respond admirably; the next day it would be Bach or Beethoven, and the response was not so good; Mozart presented further difficulties. The weather affected not only the tuning, but also the action of the instruments. Dampness would cause the wood to swell, and the notes would stick. Now that Doris was able to effect her own repairs, things became much easier, and my fears that she would tire of the new life were completely dispelled. She never played for less than four hours per day, for she had an amazing repertoire. But in addition to her music, she had now taken completely to the bush life.

Animals and insects never failed to captivate her. With her collection of seven pet dogs, two vervets, a baboon, and a leopard cub, she would often leave home before sunrise, and when on occasions she had not returned by 10 a.m. I became worried and went out to look for her. Invariably I found her with a notebook, making notes on the behaviour of ants, of which she soon learned a great deal. Termite nests she often broke down and sat for hours watching the insects reconstruct the damaged parts. Spiders, wasps, moths, and butterflies were regularly subjected to intense study, and before long she

knew more about these insects than I did.   Chameleons held a
strange appeal for her, and there were often as many as fifteen
scattered all over the house.   One of her happy moments was
when an old mother chameleon presented us with six healthy
babies one day.

After I had left the mine and again taken to a roving life in
the bush Doris accompanied me on every safari.   She was with
me during the whole of my nine months' safari in the Rift
Valley, and also on the prolonged Locust Control expedition.
On these trips conditions often became so difficult that even I
was taxed to the limit, but she accepted it all cheerfully and
always found something to amuse and interest her in the bush.
Only one thing always distressed her, and that was the killing
of animals, though she was wise enough to realize that often
there was no other way out.   Those were the occasions when
shortage of food supplies necessitated the killing, and when
dealing with animals that had become a menace to the safety
of human beings.   These killings she would accept and
tolerate, but never would she be present when the killing had
to be done.

A safari to her meant an opportunity to study another part
of the country and to admire wild life in its natural state.   On
the open plains, where game was plentiful and the country
easy to traverse by car or truck, I was left to go out alone and
replenish the meat larder.   After that many hours were spent
driving from one herd of animals to another so that she could
watch and admire the different species.   When we encountered
herds in which there were young ones present it was often
difficult to persuade her to go farther afield.

Later, when I had disposed of the Ibach Grand, we decided
to buy a smaller instrument which could be conveniently loaded
and carried with us on safaris of long duration.   Often the
instruments had to be carried by porters, when road conditions
became impossible to negotiate by motor transport.   A
humorous incident, which at the time it happened I did not
consider so funny, occurred when I went out one morning to
shoot meat for the porters before moving on to the next camp
later in the day.

I had gone out hoping to find game close to camp, but things
went all wrong and I was eventually persuaded to follow a

o

buffalo trail. It was fifty-six hours later when I finally returned to camp. During my absence I had lived through my narrowest escape ever from a charging buffalo. In fact one of my legs was actually grazed as he rushed past me in full charge.

Throughout that same night my trackers, spotters, and I were menaced by a lion, and without a spot-light I could not account for him. On at least three occasions I fully expected him to rush in and kill us all. On that hunt I nearly died from thirst and hunger, and when I struggled back to camp two days later I was so tired and weary that it was sheer agony for me to put one foot in front of another.

It was at the moment when I was approaching camp that I heard the strains of ' The Dead March ' being played on the piano. My appearance and gait probably justified Doris's choice of music at the time, but she did not know then that only a fraction of an inch had saved her from the necessity of playing ' The Dead March ' over my dead body. She herself had spent those two nights in the open with only an old cook boy and a few porters in camp, but she was not unduly upset by the experience. After the trail of the buffaloes had started I had sent back a messenger to tell her that I might be delayed for some time. The trip had so fatigued me that I had to postpone our departure for two days. During those two days I lay in bed and listened to a great artist playing Chopin, Beethoven, Mozart, Mendelssohn, and the most popular Neapolitans for hours on end. How many hunters in the far-back-blocks of Central Africa have ever enjoyed such an experience?

Doris often caused me concern by the manner in which she approached poisonous insects and reptiles. There was the occasion, already related, when I found her holding a poisonous cobra by the head and tail; a fool snake-man had mistaken it for a harmless grass snake and handed it to her. Then there were the numerous occasions on which she removed the collar from Spots, my pet leopard—now almost full grown—and allowed him to accompany her on long walks into the bush. Spots never attempted to harm her, and often returned with his tongue hanging out from thirst and fatigue after a long walk. When I found her one day teasing Spots by hanging on to his tail whilst he tried to escape, I had to put my foot down forcibly.

There was only one occasion on which I saw her really distressed in the bush. That was the day, whilst on Locust Control work, when I had received instructions to investigate the southern area of Lake Rukwa as far as the lake shores. We were camped quite 12 miles from the lake shore, and when we set out that morning the idea was that we would spend the night at the lake and return the next day. Had I known at the time that no European had ever traversed that section of the country, owing to the impossible conditions, I should have hesitated to undertake the trip on my own.

Although we left before sunrise that morning, it was nearly 3 p.m. when we arrived at our destination, to find that the entire area was infested with snakes, scorpions, and millions of mosquitoes. Far out in the distance some fool had set the grass alight, and it was essential for us to quit the area without loss of time before we were cut off by the grass fire. At that time of the year the temperature frequently rose to 120 degrees in the shade during the hottest part of the day. The 12 miles we had walked through most difficult country that morning had utterly fatigued us. Now we were compelled to face a similar ordeal to reach camp in safety.

Doris complained volubly that night when huge blisters formed on her feet, for it was after 11 p.m. before we reached camp. The gruelling strain of the day had of itself proved a most trying and wretched experience. The situation was aggravated when we straggled into camp just in time to see her beautiful Great Dane pet dog breathe his last as the result of a snake-bite. Only a few months earlier I had imported that dog at heavy cost from Uganda. Just how we ourselves escaped a similar fate that night, walking through snake-infested country in the dark, will always remain a puzzle to me.

There were many occasions when, after a successful hunt, the trackers and porters would gather round the camp-fire at night. I always preferred the Mwemba tribe for hunting; they are excellent bushmen and great humorists. One of their admirable traits is their fondness for music and singing. They often astonished me when I listened to them singing and harmonizing sacred songs and Christmas carols. With Doris at the piano, a huge camp-fire burning brightly at night, a crowd of blacks sitting singing in beautiful harmony, the setting always appeared fantastic and unreal to me.   It was a life of love, devotion, and affection in which glorious music formed part of our very existence deep in the forest.   It was to continue for ten happy years.

I think back to that memorable Christmas Eve far out on the lonely Usanga Plains.   As always at Christmas time, the camp was well supplied with meat. By 7 p.m. the camp-fire was burning brightly.   That night it was packed much higher than usual.   Already the twenty Mwembas were sitting round it; nearby stood the piano.   Doris and I had been sitting watching them piling on wood for some time when she excused herself and entered the tent.   The blacks had already started singing; there was something tense and solemn about this night.   A few moments later she reappeared, beautifully gowned in a white dinner-frock, and walked over to the piano.

For more than an hour I sat listening to the singing and music: popular melodies and Christmas carols.   That night the blacks were inspired; for all the world it might have been a well-trained chorus giving an audition.   And then, slowly, Doris struck the opening bars of ' Silent Night '.   Every native in Africa knows that melody, and that night the Mwembas were excelling themselves.   When the dying strains faded away I was stirred to the soul.   Slowly the blacks started moving from the fireside and returned home—perhaps they, too, were overcome with emotion.   After they had all gone, Doris and I sat looking out on the open plain.

From above, at intervals, through drifting clouds, a full moon poured golden beams on the valley below.   Dotted all round us were the isolated palms—those lonely sentinels with their drooping leaves.   For how many centuries have they stood there as we beheld them that night?   But never before could they have inspired a setting such as this.   I sat deep in thought, gazing and thinking of the beauty of it all.   What more could the night offer us?   Then again came the strains of soft, heavenly music.   It was Doris playing the ' Moonlight Sonata '.   After the last plaintive notes had died away, we rose, covered the piano, and returned to our tent.   It had all been so impressive, so soul-stirring, but still there was something missing. During the whole of that night no animal had given voice to complete the picture.

Then suddenly, in the distance, we heard the cry of a hyena. ' Perhaps he is hungry,' said Doris. ' Why not give him a Christmas treat and put out some meat for him to eat? ' I went out, pulled down a shoulder of venison, and threw it out in the darkness. I had hardly re-entered the tent when we heard yet another sound; it came from a long distance—a sound that was familiar to us and one we had often heard before in the still of night: the lusty roar of a male lion, far out on the open plain. But there was no menace in that sound; perhaps he too was telling the denizens of the wild that it was Christmas time and that all was peaceful and quiet— a silent night, a holy night. For a while we lay in silence, thinking of this wonderful night; then we bade each other good-night and dropped off into a peaceful sleep.

But ' it is change alone that changeth not '. This idyllic life could not last for ever. I had by now spent more than thirty years in the wilds. During all those years I had not seen my mother or any other member of my family. The bush had lost much of its appeal, as conditions were getting ever harder. Defective eyesight and the many years of strain had made serious inroads on my nerves. There came the morning when once again I escaped death by the merest fraction of an inch and one of my trackers was severely injured by a wounded bull. The incident made a deep impression on my mind, and lived with me for several days.

It was ten days later before I again felt equal to trying my luck with a buffalo. That morning we stalked a herd in close country and in due course caught up with them. Seated under a tree under perfect cover, a monster bull presented an ideal target—no more than 100 yards away. It was one of the easiest shots imaginable, and there was no reason to anticipate any untoward incident. As I raised my rifle and brought the bull into my sights, the thought suddenly came to me: ' Will there be another accident? If anything unexpected happens, will my luck again hold good? ' That was a sure indication that the steadiness of nerve and confidence, so essential in hunting dangerous animals, was on the wane. It was time to call a halt. I lowered my rifle and walked back to camp.

' Doris,' I said when I reached home, ' I have had the bush, and before long the bush will probably have had me. It is time to bring down the curtain—time to return to civilization and find something that the bush, with all its fascination, cannot provide.' She agreed with me. A fortnight later we bade adieu to the bush life for ever. We were on our way to Southern Rhodesia.

CHAPTER XXIV

THE END OF THE TRAIL

WHEN WE LEFT our camp prior to returning South, it was necessary for me to go first to Chunya, where I started mining operations on alluvial gold when I first came to Tanganyika. At Chunya I had some property to dispose of, and I had arranged for all mail to be re-addressed to me at this address whilst I was away on my last safari. On my arrival there I found three letters awaiting me. The first was from the mining company for whom I had worked as secretary, offering me the job of private secretary in Kenya. The second was an offer from the Tanganyika Government to go on another control job—this time on Rinderpest control. The third was from the Belgian Congo Government—also on Elephant control work.

The last offer seemed very lucrative, as the conditions provided that I would be supplied with all camp equipment, including rifles and ammunition. Half of the ivory shot would revert to me and, in addition, all smoked meat would be bought from me at a controlled price of four pence per lb. I figured that if I shot only 100 elephants during the first year of the contract, the ivory alone would be worth over £1,000 and the meat should return considerably more than £2,000. It was a very interesting offer, and I turned it over in my mind for a long time without being able to come to a decision.

The financial side of it was undoubtedly good, but it entailed once again the hard conditions of the bush in an unhealthy part of the country. There was, too, my natural aversion to killing elephants, and the fact stared me in the face that I was no longer so well equipped physically to inspire the necessary confidence for such dangerous work. In the end I decided to discuss the matter with Doris in full detail and abide by her decision. Her answer was, ' Fate seems to be conspiring to keep you in the bush until you come to a violent end. Only a few days ago you decided that your eyesight and nerves were no longer equal to the demands of dangerous hunting. How long will it be before these defects will lead you to tragedy? To my mind you have already played your luck far too long. Do you think it is worth while to tempt fate any further? Three thousand pounds is a lot of money, but it is of no earthly use to a dead man. Also, you have promised your mother that after thirty years' absence you would soon be returning home. It will be unkind of you to disappoint her in this.'

That was good enough for me. Although she would not put obstacles in my way if I really wanted to accept the offer, it was obvious that she was not very much in favour of it. It was true also that Mother was now well on her way towards her four-score years, and that she was longing to see me again. By that same mail there was a letter for me telling me that two of my half-brothers were doing very well on a gold-mining proposition, and that they were prepared to cede some valuable ground to me. Ten days later we arrived at Bulawayo station, where Mother and the other members of the family awaited us. That meeting was yet another emotional experience. Accompanying Mother were two young men whom I had not previously met. These were two half-brothers, who were born after my departure thirty years before. Both were married and had small families. ' Old Nick,' who, in spite of our many misunderstandings earlier in life, I had long since forgiven and hoped to meet again, had passed on a few months earlier. There were many other changes, and everything appeared strange to me. The next month Doris and I spent in resting and enjoying family life; more so, when we found there was an excellent piano in the home.

At the end of our month's rest I started in on the mining project. The property held many promising features, but, like all gold-mining, there were risks, and the preliminary work necessary to bring the property to a producing stage would have taken more time than I was prepared to put into it. By this time I had met Percy.

Percy was a graduate from the Royal School of Mines in England. He was the son of a famous inventor who registered twenty-three patents with the War Office during the First World War. Like his father, Percy was also an inventive genius, but could never find his way about in the morass of commercial enterprise. He was now busy erecting a saw-mill, which he had adorned with at least a dozen of his quaint inventions. At his present rate of progress it was obvious that senile decay would catch up with him long before he had reached production stage. At the time I met him work had been at a standstill for several weeks owing to his precarious financial position. The timber business was then flourishing, and Percy's enterprise offered excellent prospects, if only the wheels would turn.

One evening, when he was in a particularly despondent mood, and bemoaning his ' bad luck ', I suggested to him that we form a partnership. I would undertake to instal the necessary equipment to get us into production at an early date whilst he continued to work at the patents which had landed him in his present unenviable position. A fortnight later the mill was in production. I had managed to secure the essential equipment and an experienced staff to keep the wheels turning, and attended to the financial side myself, whilst Percy worked endlessly at the patents, which he assured me would make all the existing saw-mill machinery obsolete and revolutionize the milling business.

Our milling business, however, had not yet reached the stage where it could cope with the risks and expenses these patents would involve and after a while the partnership was dissolved and I carried on by myself.

It was a hard grind, and needed a tremendous lot of supervision and control. Towards the end I employed 250 native labourers, and fifteen trucks provided the transport—the main source of most of the difficulties. During the rainy season sometimes all fifteen trucks would leave in the morning and fail to return for a week from the timber forest, which was only 20 miles away. Native drivers have no soul or imagination where motor vehicles are concerned. If a truck got stuck in the mud, a foot went down hard on the accelerator and it was kept there until something happened. If the gears and propellor shafts were not completely wrecked, the truck would sink into the mud axle deep, from where it had to be extricated by teams of oxen. It was a costly and worrying business.

At the mill I had built a comfortable home and a large music-room for Doris. Whereas in the beginning I had worried that she might wish to return to her public music life, my worry now was that she would not play in public in any circumstances whatever. Every invitation for her to appear at fêtes was turned down firmly. When the two famous singers, Tito Schipa, the tenor, and Terazzi, the baritone, proposed to do a short tour of Rhodesia on their way to visit the Victoria Falls, they approached her to act as accompanist. The suggestion was turned down flat. When the leading music concern sent out recording equipment for her to do recording she refused to entertain the idea. For some reason or other, perhaps psychological, she stuck to her resolution, and nothing could induce her to change her mind. At home, however, it was different; there she would practise up to six hours daily, and play for intimate friends. Two of my employees, a violinist and a guitarist, were quite good performers, whilst I played the 'cello reasonably well. At least twice weekly we would have musical sessions by ourselves. On the other five nights of the week a selection of records provided the entertainment.

But then things began to change: the long hours of practice were gradually reduced until finally they ceased. There was nothing in her appearance to suggest that there was anything seriously wrong; she just felt tired and listless. The local doctor who examined her could find nothing wrong. At this time the only thing that interested and cheered her was letters she received regularly from her childhood friend, Hilda, in South Africa. During all the years they had kept up a regular correspondence, and I suggested to her that she should go South to her friend for a long vacation. The idea appealed to her, and we were making preparations for her departure when she complained of feeling ill one morning. I immediately took her to a specialist in town, and he suggested that she be kept under observation in hospital for a few days. It was a Saturday, and when I left her to return to the mill later that morning she appeared almost normal.

At twelve o'clock that night the phone rang in my bedroom. It was a message from the hospital, asking me to come immediately. Doris' condition had suddenly taken a turn for the worse and she had gone into a deep coma. On arrival at the hospital I found two doctors in attendance. Her condition was obviously extremely critical. Two weeks later she appeared to rally, and she was allowed to sit in an arm-chair. I spent the day with her, and we both felt hopeful that she would soon be on her way to full recovery. But just before I was due to return to the mill she complained of feeling ill again. A few minutes later she again sank into a deep coma, from which she never recovered. It was the bitter and tragic end of one more trail. Her death affected me so much that a few days afterwards I suffered a serious collapse. When, a fortnight later, I was again able to get about, my doctor urged me to leave for the coast immediately.

The following day I left for Durban—but Durban brought me nothing but loneliness. I felt that I wanted someone to whom I could talk about Doris. In Durban there was no one, and only a few days after my arrival I went to book my passage back to Rhodesia—there at least I had friends to whom I could talk. But here again fate was to step in. That afternoon I received a letter which had been forwarded on to me from home. It was from Hilda, who was living only a few miles from Durban. She had written to express her sorrow and sympathy. I had not met Hilda previously, but I felt that I knew her. Here, at last, was someone to whom I could talk about the past. I immediately got in touch with her, and two days later she arrived in Durban. Meeting someone with whom I could share my thoughts and feelings helped to relieve the strain under which I was living. But there was a great deal for me to attend to in Rhodesia, and ten days later I returned.

During the months before her final illness, Doris had often expressed a longing to get back to the bush, and in consequence I had entered into negotiations to dispose of the business. Now, on my return, I hastened to conclude the deal. A year before this I had sent a prospector to Northern Rhodesia to peg property for us in partnership. He had discovered two valuable properties in which a big mining group had become interested. At the time of Doris' death they were forcing the issue of a sale. My mental state at the time was such that I simply could not interest myself in discussing business of this nature. Just before leaving for Durban I had given my partner a power of attorney to dispose of the one property at a suggested price. After all my affairs were cleared up in Southern Rhodesia I left for the north.

When I arrived at our new headquarters late one night in pouring rain after a 1000-mile journey another shock awaited me. My partner had disposed of the main property for a tenth of the suggested price. The sale had been concluded in an attorney's office, and there was nothing I could do about it. The partnership was liquidated and I retained the remaining property. Here I did development work for two years, but at the end of that time I again became restless. The life in the bush held nothing for me. There was no Doris, no music, no companionship, and I wanted to get away from it all. A month later I sold out and once more bade farewell to the bush. But this time the break was final.

During all this time Hilda and I had kept up a regular correspondence. I had not mapped out any definite plans for the future, and I decided I would visit Durban again and call on her. On my way down to Durban I visited Johannesburg to call on a mining group with whom I had some business. I was staggered when the director of this company informed me that the property which my partner had sold so recklessly had that week changed hands for £100,000. It had turned out to be the largest and richest manganese mine in the north. It was just one more turn of the wheel of fate. I proceeded on my way to Durban, where I again met Hilda; two months later we were married.

Hilda herself had been a great traveller all her life—England, Europe, America, Australia, West Indies, etc. She also had lost both her father and mother in one year. Around us there was nothing but memories of sadness. We decided that it would be good for both of us to get away from it all and look for different surroundings in some other country. Six months later we sailed from Durban en route to the beautiful island of Majorca. As the boat sailed out of the harbour a deep sadness came over us. We were both saying farewell to our native land—who knows, perhaps for ever.

On our way to Majorca we visited Italy, the land of music and culture. Genoa left a lasting impression on my mind, for here we visited the world's most famous cemetery. Six hundred thousand bodies are entombed there, and we saw most of the outstanding statues which mark the last resting-places of dear ones who have gone before. Death, with the sorrows it brings, is depicted here in marble statues of exquisite beauty. There is the imperishable monument, dedicated to a deceased wife by a stricken husband, to commemorate a life of fifty years of happiness. The body lies deep down in the tomb, at the portals of which stands a magnificent life-size statue in marble. It is the figure of a beautiful woman as she appeared on her wedding day. Her hands are outstretched and hold a bunch of flowers which had been deposited there the day before. As we stood admiring it, lost in thought, a drooping figure approached us. His face bore an expression of deep sorrow. Reverently he knelt before the statue and murmured a prayer. The flowers were taken from her outstretched hands and replaced with fresh blooms. For a while he stood and gazed upon the beautiful countenance, and then slowly descended the stairs to the crypt below.

' How pathetic ! ' I remarked to our guide.

' Yes, pathetic as you say, signor,' he replied. ' Every day, in rain or sunshine, he brings her fresh flowers and goes down to spend an hour with her. He is wealthy, but he has isolated himself from the world. When he returns home from here, it is to live alone with his memories.'

There are many other beautiful monuments; each one speaks of the longing and love of those who have remained behind. As I stood looking at it all, my mind went back to so many of those of my friends and loved ones departed. They do not rest in surroundings as beautiful as these, for many of them have found their last resting-places under the mighty forest giants. They, too, sleep in peace.

Barcelona, that vibrant city, where we remained for several days, also left a deep impression on my mind. The masses of people, strolling along the boulevards until the early hours of the morning, seemed strange to me. Early one morning I was awakened by the drone of human voices. I looked through the window and saw hundreds upon hundreds of people standing talking in groups out in the street. ' There must have been a serious accident for all these people to gather here at this time of night,' I said to Hilda. She came to the window, and burst into laughter. She had seen this kind of thing often before.

There had been no accident. It was merely an old Spanish custom to gather in groups and talk at two o'clock in the morning.

A few days later we took the overnight boat to Majorca, the island we had chosen in which to find happiness and contentment. Here I have spent a good deal of my time to complete these manuscripts. But we have found time to admire the beauty of this ancient and historical island. The cathedral, that massive stone edifice in Palma, which took 400 years to build; the quaint, narrow streets where the amazing products of the island are displayed in neatly decorated shop windows; the ancient wall around the city; the famous Borne, with its delightful cafés and restaurants; the stately palaces with their fascinating courtyards; and then there is the Carthusian Monastery at Valldemosa, where Chopin composed some of his immortal music—music to which I listened so often on the open plains in Central Africa.

I am writing these notes on the terrace of our beautiful flat overlooking the vast expanse of the Mediterranean. Out in the bay is the overnight boat, brightly illuminated in multi-coloured lights, sailing out majestically on her way to Barcelona. All along the coastline myriads of lights are reflected on the silent water in the Bay. To the left lies the city of Palma. The shadows have deepened; in the distance stands the massive flood-lit cathedral. Yes, it is all very beautiful, and I feel that we have found what we came to seek.